INNER EMBER

MARK SANGSTER

INNER EMBER

Five Days Alone in Death Valley in Search of My Authentic Self

GFB

Published by GFB™, Seattle
www.girlfridayproductions.com

Produced by Girl Friday Productions

Cover design: Emily Weigel
Development & editorial: Audra Figgins
Project management: Sara Addicott

Image credits: Kelly vanDellen/Shutterstock (night landscape),
CreativeDoctah/Shutterstock (fire), Ravindra37/Shutterstock (embers)

ISBN (paperback): 978-1-964721-74-3
ISBN (ebook): 978-1-964721-42-2

Library of Congress Control Number: 2025926045

First edition

Land Acknowledgment

I want to acknowledge that the ancestral land we gathered on for our spiritual journey is the territory of the Timbisha Shoshone people. I recognize the Oglala Sioux for sharing their medicine and Black Elk's teachings from his vision quest. I acknowledge the culture and spirit of the Puebloan people of Taos, New Mexico, who inspired me. I also recognize the ancestral lands of the Anishinaabe, Chonnonton, and Haudenosaunee peoples, upon whose land I live and write.

Contents

Author's Note

I am writing this book nearly ten years after returning from a spiritual journey in Death Valley. It recounts my experiences alone in the desert and serves as a reminder that daily life often impedes our ability to live.

This book is a memoir, but it also describes various versions of Indigenous rituals, ceremonies, and beliefs. Consider it an opinion piece. It is in no way a guide to Native American or any other Indigenous cultural practices, which have been too often trampled by European-colonizer ideology. During my spiritual journey, I observed how my guide had an ideology of living in harmony with the land, rather than its exploitation. He demonstrated an understanding of the world as a living place and showed a deep respect for all life—a pure form of environmentalism that goes beyond recycling boxes or emissions taxes.

The journey I undertook was based on the vision quest, a specific spiritual rite of passage practiced by some Indigenous peoples. The term "vision quest" has become widely and carelessly used, leading to commercialization and misunderstanding around its sacred origins. Many Indigenous peoples consider this cultural theft.

When I was introduced to this ritual in 2013, I lacked the background to understand its origins and place in Indigenous cultures. While in Death Valley, my spiritual guide used the term "vision quest," and that's how I understood it. Now, as

I write this book in 2025, I have opted to use the terms "spiritual journey" or sometimes "wilderness quest." These terms summarize my solo experience in the desert, with its focus on inner purpose and experiencing visions, while respecting the deep spiritual heritage of the original term to which I can lay no cultural or ethnic claim. Where I use the term "vision quest," it accurately portrays a conversation that took place during my time in the desert.

Some argue that guided vision quests for non-Indigenous peoples could be considered appropriation—the theft of a cultural element or practice without permission and without an understanding of its meaning or significance and acknowledgment of its origins. At its best, appropriation leads to the commoditization of precious cultural ideals; at its worst, it perpetuates harmful stereotypes and contributes to the oppression of those communities. Appropriation is the continued dominance of a culture that is disadvantaged. It's the retail-ready version of theft, priced to move with each tourist's visit to a store selling Indigenous items alongside energy drinks and Tylenol.

In contrast, I view what I did as an act of appreciation. I studied under a white man who had learned from members of the Sioux Nation. I was there to offer respect to Indigenous cultures with an open mind for learning and an open heart for understanding. I wasn't there to steal their symbols, exploit their rite for profit (at least not monetarily), or disrespect their ways.

I sought to learn and understand Indigenous cultures and practices genuinely, and to give credit where credit is due. If anything, I hope this book fosters an interest in Indigenous cultures and their rituals, wherever you may live.

And while I should not speak for my fellow travelers, I observed a solemn respect from them for Indigenous values at all times. They, too, were seeking healing. We were there to learn and to put in the hard work to experience what Indigenous teachings might offer in terms of soulful expansion and healing. And in return, we did our utmost to respect Indigenous teachings and medicines.

I have no illusion that my experience, which included donning weather-tech clothing and ultralight camping gear designed for modern mountain climbing, enlisted me in the ranks of Native Americans who participated in authentic vision quests before me. At most, I was a visitor in their world. Nonetheless, I am eternally grateful for the wisdom and guidance that afforded me the chance to discover what I had buried deep inside me. I urge you to seek out the root sources of knowledge if you wish to learn about Indigenous cultures and their rituals. Like most facts in life today, we must check and recheck across multiple sources to determine what we can believe and which sources of information we trust.

The memories that I share here are mine; others did not document or corroborate my stories. There is no evidence. A leather-bound journal in which I kept notes, lessons, rituals, and thoughts is gone now. About a year before writing this, I burned it one night in our firepit. Ironically, I thought it no longer served me and that its energy was better used in returning to the universe. As I wrote this book, digging into my memories and the path my life has taken since then, I realized how little I understood in that moment, and how much more I still have to learn.

Some of the characters you will meet in these pages are accurate representations of real people, like Sparrow Hart. Others have pseudonyms or are amalgamations of multiple individuals to preserve individual anonymity. Regardless, their stories belong to them. What I describe is my interpretation of their experiences, where they collided with mine. I may never meet those people again, but we shared something divine. And I'm proud to have counted myself as their kin in that experience.

What I experienced sleeping under the stars was unique to me. Another traveler (as I call those who embark on this kind of spiritual journey) will see *their* visions, call in *their* darkness, and find *their* purpose. They may choose different rituals to ground and call the spirits around them. That is the beauty of this endeavor. No two travelers walk the same path. A wilderness quest does not come with a money-back guarantee or warranty. It is up to the traveler to put in the work if they wish to receive the gifts.

Much of what I detail is about the visions I received. Visions are not as they are portrayed in movies. They are neither enhanced with CGI nor intended for casual entertainment. Don't walk into the wild and expect David Attenborough to narrate some James Cameron version of your life. It's more subtle than that. Moreover, it is far more introspective. Most importantly, keep in mind that visions don't come when they are called. They come when needed and only when the traveler is ready to receive them.

INTRODUCTION

Lost

It was just another normal Saturday evening in 2024 until I received an email that would disconnect me from what I thought I knew. It was like the arc of electricity when you unplug an ungrounded appliance. In an instant, I went from happy and relaxed to shocked, confused, and then scared.

I had spent over thirty years working in technology and cybersecurity. I had built a thought-leadership practice, which led me to make appearances on CNN, to address national cyberattacks, to lecture at Harvard University on cyberthreats to the legal system, and to write two books on the subject. As one expert in the security field put it, "When Mark Sangster speaks about cybersecurity, people listen." I was at the top of my professional game. Or so I thought.

For the past few years, I'd been working for a DC-based cybersecurity firm founded by two retired National Security Agency officers. One started as a good friend, and the other had become so. I had created a similar business before, and this new venture was tracking above the curve in terms of financial growth and with lucrative exit potential if we sold the company or took it public. It was the tech dream. Decades of toiling in start-ups only to make others rich were coming to an end. I was positioned to make a significant profit off this deal. It was what I called "fuck-off money"—not enough to buy an island or luxury yacht, but enough to provide financial freedom to pick and choose what I did next. It was to be the crowning culmination of my career.

Months before, at a conference, I sat with our disheartened CEO. He seemed conflicted about selling the company to a larger tech firm that had made an offer. Investors were more aggressive than usual after the COVID-19 economic downturn. The amount of funding we required to continue operations would dilute the stock and potentially reduce the amount of money shared among the employees.

"Look, this sale is pretty good," I said. Drawing on experience with a similar deal, I was familiar with the alternatives. And it was a painful climb over the trench walls of the spreadsheets and the unrealistic expectations of private equity and heavy-hitting investors. Even if we toiled for another few years at the risk of personal burnout, we'd likely see the same return.

"Take the offer in hand, and we will make it work." I wanted to help dispel his indecision. "And if there isn't a role for me and other execs when it closes, well, we will manage," I offered as an absolution from any personal guilt he might be feeling. But he knew more than he was saying.

Weeks later, we were deep in negotiations and nearing the conclusion of the sale of the company. I was also negotiating my new employment contract with the buyer. My family was watching TV together after dinner on Saturday evening when I checked my phone. I saw an email from the acquiring company. "We revoke your offer," it read. The rest of the email contained euphemisms, rice-paper thin, disguising promises they likely never intended to keep.

In a handful of bytes, I had gone from a deal-written-in key player to another unemployed statistic. What had promised to be a lucrative deal for me, in terms of a significant financial payout and a new job with the company, now meant I would be unemployed when the deal closed. No payout was coming my way.

Like a deep cut, the shock turned from panic and disorientation to one of lost safety. In an instant, I was transported back to my childhood. I was eight, amusing my younger brother, who was seated in a shopping cart as my parents paid for our Friday-night groceries. I looked forward to my favorite cereal, which I would eat the following morning while watching cartoons on TV. The manager came over and refused to honor my parents' check. It seemed they had bounced one too many before and were on a watch list. "Cash only, sir," the manager said.

I played dumb and focused on my brother, who was oblivious to our predicament. My parents' humiliation radiated like a light bulb, and I was not going to add to it—each dealt with their indignity in their way.

My mother picked over the groceries to preserve the essentials. She was triaging our food for the week. Her shaking hands gave away her emotions as she desperately dug through her purse to scrounge enough cash to cover the purchase, almost begging the lint and broken lipsticks to surrender any hidden coins or bills.

As the other customers in line behind us looked on, my father held his ground, arguing with the manager. His negotiation was pointless, and he was aware of it. It was a pantomime of indignation to save face in front of an impartial audience now impatient with the resulting delay. Some customers glared and grumbled unintelligible grievances, while others stared at imagined focal points, too embarrassed for our family to make eye contact. The young cashier counted the money while the manager looked on, as if he were the boss overseeing some high-stakes game at a casino table. With our remaining cash secured in the till, the cashier and manager hastily bagged the meager groceries, like we were lepers to be feared. We left, our tails between our legs.

I said nothing, pushing the cart toward our car. I dreaded my Saturday morning. The altercation with the manager had cost me a precious moment of simple childhood bliss. But I had lost more than that. I had lost my sense of fundamental safety. This was another tremor forecasting the mounting pressure toward a volcanic explosion of domestic violence. I'd have to endure a protracted Friday night of fear before I could enjoy my Saturday-morning cartoons.

The memory faded, and I was back in my own living room, facing my bewildered family. "Babe, can you read this email? Does it say what I think it does?" I asked my wife, Michelle. She sat silently, reading and rereading the message on my phone. "Yes, I think it does. They just fired you when the deal closes," she confirmed.

Our confusion and shock bounced around the room as our daughters became aware of our distress. We explained what we were reading and its meaning. My eighteen-year-old, Rebecca, looked up from her phone as her stepsister, Lauren, a twenty-seven-year-old who visited frequently, paused the TV program. Lauren was my wife's child. We'd each brought a child into our blended second marriage.

Lauren went to guns, with an expletive-filled rally cry for lawsuits and court battles, while Rebecca, still in university, lacked the work experience to make sense of the situation. She was bewildered. We all were.

My family was supportive. We loved one another. They were furious on my behalf. When I considered the commitment and sacrifices I'd made for this job, it was my family who had paid the heaviest toll—years of my travel and absence had accrued a return of less than zero. Their sacrifice in terms of an absent father and their investment in missed family moments was nothing but a loss. For them, it was a betrayal in which I was an active participant. They were not mad at me; they, too, were hurt. Whatever the payout was supposed to be, it had not materialized.

I had spent more than a decade traveling around the globe to do what I did best, but this email meant the end of the road. I would no longer speak at international conferences or on TV to mesmerized audiences. I was no longer the veteran expert telling stories of elaborate cybersecurity fraud. No more briefing government agencies or helping high-level executives protect their businesses. Because I didn't have a job, no one would come seeking my help. Had my clever metaphors, lessons, and polished presentations become a thing of the past? Had I dropped the microphone for the last time? At fifty-seven, it was a good possibility.

It stung, too, because I enjoyed the influence and notoriety I'd created. I enjoyed the travel. I had always wanted to climb Mount Everest, and my career had become my mountain. Each progressive role or promotion was another base-camp stay on my way to the summit.

In an instant, a simple email message had knocked me off my peak, and I was falling without a harness. I tried to control my sense of dread. We were financially secure and better off than most families. Regardless, that old wound of childhood insecurity tore open and spilled anger and fear into my mind. I was afraid of what was to come, and I was unsure of my future. In an instant, I knew I had let my family down. I was echoing the path of my father, though I was negotiating not with a store manager but the universe to keep my family fed and safe.

As I sat in disbelief, a profound throbbing replaced the

initial stabbing pain. And the days that followed transformed pain into anger at the betrayal and reversal of fortune, which melted into an aching within me. This cut had penetrated deeply enough to rip open an inner wound. It curled up in a fetal position as I gently sobbed.

My wife gave me the room to grieve rather than panicking into any job before figuring out what the next thing should look like. The last thing she wanted to witness was my rush into another drastic decision without first understanding the problem I was trying to solve.

"Honey, rather than just finding another job, take the time to consider what you *want* to do," she advised me. "I know you're scared." She paused and made me look into her eyes. "We are safe." She chanted it like a mantra. "We have money, and the house is paid for." As she continued, I knew she was talking to that little boy in the grocery store.

Michelle was right. I was running from one thing to the next. I was constantly seeking the next dopamine hit. I needed to stop valuing my life simply by my career, rank, or exposure. I needed to fill more than a void. I needed to rekindle what excited me. Did I want to go back to a life measured by hotel memberships and airline-loyalty miles? It was time to put down my old life and contemplate a new one.

I'd received the news just before Christmas, so I postponed my job search and took some time to enjoy the holidays. I would take the space my wife offered and just be. The all-consuming merger, relegated to the rearview mirror, meant I had the mind, space, and energy to immerse myself in a time of year that our family held special.

Five years ago, we had purchased a house just off the highway, and in good traffic, it was forty-seven minutes from the Toronto airport. But now its proximity to my travel gateway was less important. Michelle had found the house, and we'd bought it as much as an investment as a refuge. Located as we were on a cul-de-sac, we intentionally used the yard to build a cottage in the city, installing a pool, investing heavily in landscaping and trees, and building a firepit large enough for ten people to sit around.

That December, it snowed nearly every day, promising a white Christmas. I was relaxed in a way I had not been in years. One night, I slipped out of the house and traced a giant happy face in the snowy canvas of our cul-de-sac. I basked in our neighborhood's multicolored lights and holiday displays. I inhaled the cold air and felt warm in the moment.

On Christmas Eve, I stayed up after everyone else went to bed and wrapped my wife's gift. It was a small artisan ring with a moonstone gem. I placed the ring box in a small, discarded Amazon box. Then, I wrapped that box. I went back to our recycling and found a slightly larger box. In the gift went. I wrapped progressively larger boxes until the ring sat cocooned in something that resembled a camping cooler, nestled in reindeer paper. I giggled at my handiwork. It was the first time in a long time that I had indulged in a wasteful act of amusement that I would have previously rejected as an unnecessary mess.

I watched the black-and-white adaptation of *A Christmas Carol* starring Alastair Sim. I felt like the reborn Ebenezer Scrooge on Christmas morning, reveling in the childlike magic of the holiday. I set out a plate of carrots for the reindeer, and cookies with a glass of milk and a dram of whisky for Santa. Our kids were young adults, but the magic dies only when you stop believing. And they still appreciated the magic.

Christmas and then the new year came. I packed away the festive trimmings, and the absence of holiday lights and golden baubles created a suffocating vacuum. *What now?* I thought. Everyone else had returned to school or work, and I had nowhere to go and nothing to do. January suddenly felt empty and bland, and I was deflated.

I spent time contacting colleagues and asking "What's

next?" It was half hearted. I was not ready for what was next. I was not over what had been. I'd send some emails, take a quick call, and pretend I was okay. I quickly ran out of chores and tasks to keep my mind occupied. January slipped out the front door unnoticed.

One morning in February, I stood on the scale, staring at the number in disappointment. Though I'd been a gym devotee, I had been slipping. No amount of sucking in my gut could convince those little numbers to change. Worse, my reflection told me the weight was more than physical. It was emotional. And perhaps something more. *Forget what you gained,* my eyes told me. *Think of what you have lost.*

I had always dreamed of seeing the world. I was inspired at a young age when my mother took me to the Royal Ontario Museum to see the Tutankhamen exhibit. The art of ancient Egypt enthralled me. I longed to see the pyramids. I loved the idea of backpacking and adventuring across Europe and Australia and completing walks like the Camino de Santiago pilgrimage through France and Spain. Born in Scotland before emigrating to Canada at a young age, I felt a detachment from where I lived and always believed that other places could teach me and share something more about life, nature—anything. Scotland was economically depressed in the late sixties and early seventies, and places like the United States, Canada, and Australia held a promise of self-made prosperity. It was not that I disliked Canada. On the contrary, I am a proud Canadian, but I sometimes still feel like a stranger in my land.

I have always been drawn to the mountains, watching documentaries about scaling Everest, K2, or El Capitan in Yosemite. When I traveled on business, I often brought my hiking boots and hit the trails in Nevada or Arizona. I'd spend a few extra days driving to Taos, New Mexico, or offbeat towns nearby, just to explore.

In my free time, I started thinking about all this. It was a pang, almost like a feeling of intense hunger. I thought back to the trip I took into the Death Valley desert after my father passed away in 2012. I had spent five days alone without food or shelter—and it had been life changing.

I felt something small spark inside me, as though someone was blowing on cold ashes, causing a small ember to reignite and glow. It was a sensation of belonging and purpose beyond something as corporeal as a job. I felt a sense of creativity surge. "Hello, little friend," I said to this feeling, this inner ember, glowing again for the first time in a long time. "Where have you been?"

I was filled with an intrinsic knowing that I could contribute to something bigger than a single life or person. It was the same sense of rightness of being I had experienced when I looked after my younger brother, who was severely disabled, or when I painted with oils and acrylics.

Everyone has an inner ember. It is the feeling of pure joy. It is a certainty that what you are doing is aligned with your own highest good. It is serendipity confirming that everything is clicking into place as it is meant to. Your inner ember connects you to a power beyond worldly concerns; you might call it God or Gaia or Spirit—whatever you prefer.

Your inner ember is your compass toward gratitude. Moreover, your inner ember, like that of a fire, flits for a moment and lives in that singular experience. Embers are not the fire itself. They are little dancing fairies of light and warmth that float up to become one with the stars. Like stars, your inner ember helps you navigate your path. But like any ember, it needs to be fed. Without oxygen, it will become cold and dim.

That solo trip in the desert had fed my inner ember, and it had glowed stronger than any other time I could remember. Cold and alone, I'd spent days fasting to commune with the universe. I'd sought energetic medicine to heal from old wounds, to help me find purpose, and to connect with a community of people worthy of my gifts.

At that point in my life, I had been looking for answers that I could not hear, that had been drowned out by the cacophony of everyday life. My thoughts had taken center stage while I was alone in the desert. I had to face my past and my fears without distraction. It was in this solitude that I realized my first marriage was over and my career was derailing. Acknowledging those monumental truths had been the first step on my new path forward—a path that led to the success and happiness I later built with Michelle and our merged family.

But now, in 2025, unemployed and feeling profoundly untethered from purpose, it was clear I had circled back to that moment when I'd first decided to go into the desert. And I realized that my inner ember had been fading for a while, even before that fated email.

Now, my inner ember was too dim even to show me what direction I should go. My job was gone, and I was in the darkness. I wanted to retrace my steps to the last place I remembered feeling whole. I wanted to return to the desert.

My trip to the desert had not been a trivial, spur-of-the-moment undertaking. It had been meticulously planned by an expert experienced in this kind of wilderness quest, who had helped many people through the process. He called it a "vision quest," a term coined by non-Native anthropologists to describe a coming-of-age rite originated by Indigenous peoples such as the Anishinaabe of the Great Lakes region, the Inuit of the Arctic (including Alaska, Canada, Greenland, and Russia), the Lakota across the Great Plains, and the Pueblo peoples of the southwestern United States, among many others (see Author's Note).

This rite of passage was a way of communing with Spirit to seek guidance or purpose. Guided by elders and supported by their tribe, the youth would spend four or so days alone in a sacred wilderness site. They prayed to and communicated with the spirits to receive a vision of their purpose in life and their role in the larger community.

Alone in Death Valley, my inner ember had glowed. Now, standing in my bathroom, stripped bare, I realized what I had lost: my connection to something more than a job. I had lost my connection to Source.

I consider Source to be the origin of everything, from existence to consciousness. It's the energy that connects all things. It's where we come from before birth and that which we return to in death. It's a spiritual north that guides us toward something more than basic human existence, something bigger that plays at a scale beyond our comprehension. It is at once light, purpose, and existence. Source is my interpretation of something bigger. It is perhaps our creator, the omnipotent being who welded the necessary elements of life. Or it's the cosmic interconnected energy of all things. It's where we come from and where we return when we die. Whether it is heaven after our time on earth or literally ashes to ashes, molecules to molecules, it is an energy that connects all things. It's the harmonic resonance of a stable state of being.

Source goes by many names and appears in many forms. Many Indigenous cultures (like the Algonquians and Lakota) call it the Great Spirit; Abrahamic religions call it God and worship their deity in return for eternal salvation. Even the apparent antithesis of faith, science, glances at its periphery with quantum physics and the Newtonian laws of conservation of mass and energy.

In terms of conservation, matter and energy cannot be created or destroyed; they can only be transformed. They can only be changed from one form to another. We live and then return to the earth from which we came—ashes to ashes, molecules, and atoms. Death is simply life's energy transforming to some other form, as the matter of the deceased body decays to be used in some other way. Nothing is lost; it's simply changed.

When it comes to miracles and the unbelievable, religion has nothing on quantum physics. This field of study is more mysterious than any theology, given its mind-bending concepts and predictions of unbreakable connections that span immeasurable distances across space and time, and even infinite dimensions. Albert Einstein himself treaded carefully around quantum physics, calling aspects of its laws "spooky." As science reveals more, it increasingly employs terminology more suitable for faith-based beliefs.

Regardless of language, both religion and science express the same concept of finite participation in an infinite universe. We emerge from Source and return to it. Whether this form of eternity is described as heaven or the laws of conservation, it is a way of comprehending eternity.

Whether Source, God, or the cosmos provides a moral compass is another question altogether. Most churches would have us believe so. But I think it is more subtle than that. It is about creation rather than morality. Creativity is the act of bringing forth order from chaos. As Michelangelo is attributed to saying, "I saw the angel in the marble and carved until I set him free." He didn't question whether carving an angel was right or wrong. Likewise, the wolf doesn't consider the morality of killing its prey. And likely the prey doesn't think the wolf is evil; it runs from the wolf out of an evolved sense of self-preservation. The wolf hunts for sustenance based on its evolved instincts. With enough sustenance, it procreates. Destruction leads to creation. Nothing is lost; it is only transformed.

Life on a cosmic scale is not about right or wrong on the individual scale. It's about creation and resilience on a cosmic scale. Morality is a social construct. It's an important one, but not for discussion here.

Creation is never stronger than when all things are in balance. Like in an orchestra, each musician could fight for center stage, leading to discordance, or play in harmony to perform a symphony. It's the same in life. Find your balance to open your creative potential. And in doing so, you move closer to Source.

Where has my ember gone? I wondered. *How have I drifted so far from Source?* I thought back to Death Valley. I had been a different man back then. I had a light that drew people to me. I was alive and living for purpose and meaning. In contrast, in recent years, I'd survived on a drip feed of audience applause and admiration, one conference at a time. I had slipped into inauthenticity. I had traded real light for artificial glare. I had traded family time for the praise of strangers.

My inner ember was firing again. I watched movies like *Into the Wild*, which is about Christopher McCandless's disappearance in 1992. He donated his savings, abandoned his belongings, and walked away from his life, traveling from Mexico to Alaska. He turned his back on societal norms, which he believed had poisoned his soul. I read Cheryl Strayed's *Wild*, about finding meaning in loss through a challenging trek along the Pacific Crest Trail, and Paul Theroux's *The Mosquito Coast*, about escaping the hypocrisy of society for a purer and more honest life. I watched *The Way*, a fictional story about a father who walks to the Cathedral of Santiago de Compostela in northwest Spain, after his son dies in the mountain passes of the Pyrenees. Throughout the movie, the father faces his son's death to reveal a zest for life he had given up on years ago.

It was clear I was trying to rekindle the feeling I'd had in the desert. I was diving headlong into these movies and books to search for what was in my heart all along. But my inner ember was just too dim to see.

It flickered but would not ignite in the same way it had so many years ago. I meditated in a fumbling effort to regain who I was when I came out of the desert in 2012. How much did wishful interpretations prompt actual memories? Had I truly experienced something profound in Death Valley? Did I get nothing from the desert—or worse, did I forget the message I had received there?

When you feel your inner ember glow, you know you are going in the right direction toward what matters. I knew I had to return to the last place I'd felt its presence if I wanted to find it again. I had to retrace my steps. I had to return to the desert.

At fifty-seven, I was not going to sling on a heavy pack and starve myself in solitude among the chollas and coyotes. Besides, my wife would kill me before I set one foot out our front door toward the gaping mouths of desert predators. If I could not return to the desert in body, I had to return in mind. That was the only way to reclaim my spirit, I decided.

This book is my attempt to revisit what I discovered on a dusty butte in Death Valley over a decade ago. I have drawn from surviving notes, travel receipts, related emails, and memory. It's my interpretation of those events; of course, I have lost some details to time, and some recollections might not be as accurate as they could be. But the sentiment, or spirit, of this book is authentic.

It is the story of my spiritual journey. I hope you feel a little spark from your inner ember as you read it.

PART ONE

Departure

CHAPTER ONE

Searching for Answers

Death Valley, California, Day X

I was lost and I'd just collapsed in a dust heap on the side of an unfamiliar jagged desert hill in Death Valley. I hadn't eaten in days. Without food, my routine morning hike was too much for my depleted body. My right ear was ringing, and the dust storm my tumble had created settled back around me, painting a body outline as if I were the victim in some arid crime scene.

What am I doing here? I wondered, not for the first time. Was I confused by my predicament or by the entire notion of staying alone in a place named for its deadly history? I spat the dust from my mouth and brushed the back of my gloved hand across my face. My walking stick was still tethered to my wrist, but when I raised my arm again, I saw the stick was broken.

I tried to sit up, but it felt like glass shards were sloshing around in my skull like a snow globe of agony. Confusion was pushed aside by pain.

My knee cried out as I surveyed my body for injury and blood. Broken bones could be splinted, but blood was a wilderness billboard advertising wounded prey. It was a neon arrow pointing to an easy meal for a mountain lion or coyote. I had already seen paw tracks around my encampment and knew such predators were lurking. I was now on their menu.

I remembered a story my guide had talked about: three people who had died on a spiritual retreat after spending three days alone in the Arizona desert in 2009. The victims had returned from their fasting journey to participate in a nontraditional sweat lodge. The operator, James Arthur Ray, a non-Native American, was found guilty of causing their deaths through negligent homicide. No evidence was presented that Ray had any training in Indigenous rituals, including vision quests, fasting, or sweat lodges. Native American and First Nations experts criticized Ray for conducting a fraudulent ceremony and for his ignorance and misrepresentation of actual Native American traditions.

My guide had studied and was well trained in Indigenous rituals. Yet, as I lay helpless in the dirt, miles from wherever he was, I wondered if I was fated to become a footnote on some Wikipedia page about deaths during spiritual ceremonies.

Why had I hiked miles into Death Valley and starved for days as an offering to some unnamed higher power in the hope that it would help me find answers? So far, I had nothing to show for it except physical pain and exhaustion. All the warnings from family and friends came back in waves, like a chorus of *I told you so.*

I lay my head back on my pillow of sand. The heat of the day was growing, yet I shivered. For the first time, alone in this unforgiving place, I surrendered my last snippet of control. Sweat quickly evaporated from my forehead. My guts tightened, not from hunger but from fear. I was alone and a day or two from help, assuming my companions could even find me.

It seemed as good a time as any to surrender. "You win, universe," I said to no one in particular. I looked up at the azure sky, a stark contrast to the perpetual browns and tans of the landscape. I spat more grit from my mouth, not sure what to do next and too exhausted to try.

—

Kitchener-Waterloo, Ontario, Before

About a year before my trek in the desert, my father, Bryan, died one month shy of his seventieth birthday. He'd called me earlier that spring to tell me he had been diagnosed with stage IV cancer.

"I don't want you to worry, but I was having trouble swallowing." He paused as if to prove his ailment. "After some tests, it seems I have esophageal cancer," he stoically announced. I held the phone to my ear as if it were a touchstone to keep me steady as the ground melted away underneath me.

I said nothing. This ordinary day was turning into what would become a grim milestone.

"But I don't want you to worry about me," he repeated like a half-hearted mantra. "I am going to fight this."

Like most newly anointed cancer patients, his optimism and fortitude defied the morbidity rates he would have to overcome and the reality of war that medicine was about to wage on his body at the cellular level. As I listened, not knowing what to say, he continued with promises and feigned optimism. "I have a specialist, and I will go through chemo or radiation treatment, whatever it takes to beat this."

He calmly gave me a matter-of-fact replay of his appointment with the cancer specialist, and I jumped onto Google to learn more about his diagnosis. The news was not good. Unfortunately, secondary symptoms do not appear until esophageal cancer is in later stages and are much more challenging to treat. Most patients die within a year of diagnosis. While cancer medicine promises peace, it uses debilitating poison and radiation to battle malignant growths. In my father's case, the cancer would eventually block his throat and prevent him from eating. He would starve and wither as his cancer slowly ate him from the inside.

"I know, Dad," I eventually squeaked out. "I will help you however you need." My promise was hollow. We both knew there was nothing practical I could lend, other than to participate in a march toward his demise. We had a tumultuous relationship—to say the least—and his diagnosis was one more test of our weak bonds. At that moment, he was being as brave for himself as he was for me. It's incredible how in life-changing moments, we have little more than empty promises and agreed-upon storylines to ease the fears of the dying and distract those who remain behind.

He had led a life drowned in alcohol and obscured in cigarette smoke, so I'd long wondered whether he would die prematurely of cancer or something equally self-inflicted. But even the expected can shock you by its timing. The inevitable never seems immediate. Or convenient, for that matter.

Two months later, my father had a stroke while in a taxi on the way to the hospital for an oncology appointment. The taxi driver dropped him off at the emergency room, where doctors left him unattended in the hospital hallway for seventeen hours. Further testing and examinations uncovered three golf-ball-size tumors at the base of his skull. Radiation treatment shrank the tumors, which reduced the pain and possibility of hallucinations, but the resulting nausea and weakness were unforgiving on his body.

To cheer him up during treatments, I brought my then-five-year-old daughter, Rebecca, to visit him in the hospital. She stayed amused by watching the ambulance helicopters coming and going like orange worker bees. She was equally oblivious to the drama associated with each arrival below her on the hospital landing pad and the pain and regret on display in the room with her grandfather.

A few months later, his cancer spread to his kidneys, stomach, and adrenal glands. He was transferred to palliative care. My father was drowning in morphine because the physical pain was too much to manage. The only difference between most of his prior life and his current situation was that this prescription was administered by trained medical staff rather than a bartender pouring glasses of regret. He slipped in and out of consciousness. The last time he saw me, he was agitated in a way I could not decipher. He used all his strength to point toward the corner of the room and grunt and gesture. He wanted me to understand something important, my inner ember told me. Still, I could not focus on what he could see or what he wanted me to know.

"Dad, what's there?" I asked.

He continued to gesture.

"Do you need the nurse?"

He grunted and shook his head. "No."

I looked again at the empty corner. It was near neither the door nor the medical equipment nor the bathroom. "Are you cold? Do you need a blanket?"

Again, he shook his head to the contrary.

There was a bag of items beside the bed. It was not in his line of gaze, but I tried anyway. "Do you want your bag?" No, his gestures said. "Is there something for me?"

No, his frustration indicated.

"Is someone there?" I bravely asked, fearing the answer. My ember glowed.

His response was more emphatic, and his eyes widened.

"Dad, what do you see? Are you scared?" We were on the right track, but by now, he was exhausted, and his grunts faded as his arm slowly lowered to his chest.

My father never showed much interest in religion and always wanted a low-key funeral. He didn't care about absolution or some ritual granting eternal salvation. Yet his gesturing toward an unseen entity or some invisible focal point seemed to shake him. Whatever it was, it was real, at least to him. Repeatedly, he struggled to impart his meaning to me, and then his arm would fall back to his side, and his head would fall back onto the pillow. Exhausted by the effort, he would sleep. Every time he gestured, that little ember inside me glowed brighter as if fanned by an invisible source. That was what haunted me the most.

I was not religious, but somewhere inside me, a spiritual fuse was waiting to catch fire. I was not anti-God, though I was against organized religion and its paradoxical history of suffering and atrocities that paved a path of moral guidance toward the promise of eternal peace. My analytical mind questioned the concept of an afterlife or soul, yet my spiritual inner ember reminded me to keep an open mind on matters of life and what came after it.

The following day, my father died. I got the call while standing with my daughter at the school bus stop.

"You need to come now," the palliative nurse urged.

I'd heard that before. I'd spent months going back and forth between Kitchener and London, Ontario. I had a busy workday ahead of me, and the school bus was late.

"I will get there as soon as I can." My tone suggested I was not taking her seriously enough. "I just need to put my daughter on her bus to school, and then I will head to the hospital," I said, as if I were planning a shopping trip and not trying to witness the final moments of a loved one.

Neighbors and other parents surrounded me, all of us waiting to see our kids board the bus. One father I knew well coughed as he shuffled his feet, as if to drown out the awkward conversation he was witnessing.

"Please come as soon as you can," the nurse said. When the line went dead, it punctuated the finality of the circumstances. I looked at my mobile phone, numbing myself with disregard as I focused on the task at hand.

A nearby mother, whom I also knew well, approached me. "We can put Rebecca on the bus," she offered. "You should go."

Suddenly, the magnitude of loss hit me. Tears welled up. "Okay," I whimpered. In that moment, my daughter was oblivious. She was playing with her friends, and she couldn't have cared less if I left or stayed.

I looked at Rebecca. "Hey, honey, Claire is going to put you on the bus. Daddy has to go."

"Okay, Daddy," she acknowledged, unbothered. She didn't look up from her toys.

"Thanks," I muttered to the group of parents as I walked away. The fathers looked down at their feet, fearing they might meet emotions in the others' faces, while the mothers wore their sympathy in plain sight. I started walking back up the street to my house.

The nurse had said he didn't have long, and she'd been correct. I was too late. When I arrived, he was a husk, lying in the bed. I guess he'd finally found the destination he'd sought many times before through suicide attempts, bad choices, and their resulting humiliations.

I was in shock, but missing his last moments on earth didn't seem to faze me. I was still contemplating what I had witnessed while I'd sat with him the night before. What had he seen in the corner? Who or what had been there? Or had he been hallucinating?

There are moments in your life that shake you. They do

not so much haunt you as follow you, always stealing some of your attention from the periphery. They worry away at you and never let you settle. That was when I started exploring the notion of Spirit, something more significant or beyond our comprehension that perhaps held the meaning of it all. I was moving from a judgmental resentment of religion to a path of seeking purpose in the spiritual as a member of one of the millions of species inhabiting our planet. It was an existential purpose, driven by a specific moment, that gave a glimpse of something beyond what our corporeal senses can comprehend.

I turned my back on Christianity and began exploring the gentler religions of South Asia. Hinduism and Buddhism seemed appealing. But it was in Taos, New Mexico, that I discovered a palatable flavor of Spirit. Years back, I visited a pueblo and was taken by a culture that saw the world and its inhabitants as bound together, each with a purpose, dependent on one another. No one person or species was superior. Every animal, plant, or person had intrinsic value, or "medicine," that could heal the tribe. Alternatively, every creature could poison its kin or the land when its shadow, or darker self, took control.

When I searched for sources of enlightenment regarding Native American societies, I found that most books were written by Europeans playing the part of the anthropologist, interpreting aboriginal cultures and rituals through a lens of a completely different ideological background. These Europeans were proxies in a world that had robbed the Native people of their land and way of life. The irony is that by the Europeans' very act of promoting Indigenous peoples, they ultimately robbed them of their own voice. It was the final gesture of colonialism to tell the story of the people they conquered instead of giving them a stage upon which to tell it themselves.

However, I was interested in learning about these cultures,

so I read what was available. I found Frank Waters's *Book of the Hopi*, as well as *The Book of the Vision Quest* by Steven Foster. As I read, my inner ember glowed. It was like the child's game of "Hot or Cold," in which things that brought me closer to what I later called Source would ignite that ember and glow hot.

I realized that the drudgery of professional life and the pursuit of wealth and success had driven me farther from Source. Each raise or promotion only dimmed my inner ember. I was a senior executive in an up-and-coming security firm and a celebrated speaker and author. But what did all that lead to? What did it mean? Indigenous peoples lived *with* the land, not just on it. Things were not the spoils of war to be collected. Anything good was medicine, and anything harmful was poison. Hoarding resources soured the medicine, making it poisonous. They lived in harmony with the animals and the seasons, in synchronicity with the world around them. These people were closer to Source than any European-based ideology or cultural pursuit of money and materialism.

During my research and reading, I stumbled across a shamanic practitioner, a white man who, like me, questioned society and how modern culture urged us to live. He was like many people of his generation. Sparrow Hart had grown up during the Vietnam War and was disillusioned with his country and the values it cherished. He abandoned his successful academic career and hiked the Pacific Crest Trail to look for a more meaningful path. Yet he found himself disheartened and disconnected.

Years later, Sparrow Hart wrote about his journey in his book *The Vision Quest: A Guide's Training Manual*. Sparrow Hart recalls reading John G. Neihardt's transcription of the stories told in *Black Elk Speaks*, in which a Lakota holy man describes Native American vision quests and his encounters with the grandfathers of his world. Reading those lessons struck a deep chord in Sparrow Hart. Did his inner ember burn brighter at that moment? I wondered.

Inspired, Sparrow Hart hiked to Black Elk Peak in the Black Hills of South Dakota. He sat atop the sacred mountain for days, praying through the night, soaked from the constant rain. Days without sleep or food opened a gateway to an out-of-body experience. Finally, the moon chased the clouds away, and he found what he sought. He wrote, "My boundaries dissolved as I became the mountain, and soon I was part of everything."

As he hiked back down the mountain, he knew he'd been given a gift: "I knew Spirit had spoken to me in some language I did not understand, and deep in my being, I was sure that understanding was crucial to my life." Sparrow Hart knew that engaging with the process of vision quests, or leading them, was a significant part of his journey.

When I read his book in 2019, my thoughts drifted back to my dying father, his gesturing, and my inability to decipher his message. He, too, had been speaking to me, although I could not understand what he'd been trying to tell me. Like Sparrow Hart, I knew understanding that moment was crucial to my life. I had to follow his path and understand the message my father had delivered to me.

Somehow, that understanding was the connection I craved. My ember implored me to shed life's material anchor, walk into the desert (to which I had always been drawn), and connect to Source. I wanted to know whether there was something more than me—something more than nine-to-five jobs and something of more value than money. Like Sparrow Hart, I was disheartened by our world.

The world's ember was dimming, starved of connection. Many modern cultures have transitioned from living in harmony with the land to exploiting it to fulfill our disconnected goals. We moved from a tribe of belonging to a mob determined to dominate all around us. We shifted from trading worthwhile skills and services (like blacksmithery, animal husbandry, or tailoring) to trading in representations of value—gold or silver. Paper proxies later replaced these metals, and now paper is being replaced by digital currency. Each evolutionary step was a betrayal of our existence. Somehow, the proxy became the purpose, not simply a representation of something more substantial.

As we in North America became more affluent, we did so by bankrupting our spiritual well-being. To me, attending church on Sunday and participating in transactional confessions seemed like unworthy deposits that could not remedy a balance sheet inked red with societal excesses, that condoned corporate cruelty and indifference toward the world's suffering. Humankind had traded the eventual infinite for the immediate finite. We squandered the cosmos for a title deed to a plot of land. I craved something more than a proxy. I wanted authenticity. I was seeking the source of all things, not another flashy car or big house. Once you realize the Joneses are heading in the wrong direction, there is no point in keeping up with them.

Beyond career and financial security, I was in a long-term marriage that seemed to pinball from one bad decision to the next. It was a parade of one escalation after another, designed to correct the previous round of bad mistakes.

I married my first wife shortly after graduating from university. I'd lived in residence much of my time at school, which created a social network of friends and neighbors. After graduating, I lived alone in a small apartment. My self-confidence eroded quickly. Then I met my wife where we both worked part-time in retail.

We quickly moved in together and cohabitated in a common-law relationship for years. It seemed marriage was simply another expected milestone in life. You go to school, get a job, and settle down. It was a calculated euphemism for giving up on your dreams to become a worker bee in our hive society. That was my cynical view.

I did my part. Not by choice, but perhaps through indecision. I found a nice girl, and we got married. I did love her, but it felt like settling—not with her, but with myself. It felt safer than being on my own. It was selfish, and she deserved more. When we had our daughter, Rebecca, I was a devoted father to a young girl and a rather lousy husband to her mother.

The next piece of the puzzle slotted into place when a close friend gave me a copy of *Soulcraft: Crossing into the Mysteries of Nature and Psyche* by Bill Plotkin, a psychologist who helped people on wilderness-vision fasts in the American Southwest. I read the book, called my friend, and said, "I'm going to the desert!" My ember was burning brightly as I announced the news.

I contacted Sparrow Hart and signed up for a ten-day trip to Death Valley. I was going to climb my sacred mountain and find my source. I would feed my ember.

I planned to go in March of the following year. The temperatures would still be relatively cooler than in the high summer, and I hoped the likelihood of encountering wild creatures like rattlesnakes and scorpions would be lower. I told my wife, friends, and colleagues about my plan. I was met with everything from rage to a lack of understanding to frat-boy comments designed as much to ridicule me as to shelter those intimidated by such an undertaking.

At that moment, my wife knew our marriage was over. We had been fighting for years and sleeping in separate bedrooms. She intuitively knew that her on-paper husband would enter the desert and a stranger, her future ex, would return. We had bounced close enough to divorce a few times; neither of us dared to do it. But this trip was different. I was committing to something she didn't understand. But it was a commitment.

That in itself was a harbinger of change. My daughter was too young to understand beyond the fact that Daddy was leaving on a trip to the desert. Later, she told me she had worried because she had overheard the adults talking about snakes, spiders, and other creatures from her nightmares.

Sparrow Hart recommended I prepare by reading a copy of *The Trail to the Sacred Mountain*, a guide to fasting and vision quests by Steven Foster and Meredith Little. I also studied Sparrow Hart's *Letters to the River: A Guide to a Dream Worth Living*. Those books (along with a packing list) were not only guidebooks but talismans that would see me both up the mountain and back down safely again.

I purchased a hand-tooled leather journal and began keeping notes and thoughts that would eventually help refine my purpose for this quest. I wrote about dreams, ideas, insights, encounters with animals, and anything else I overintellectualized into ammunition for my journey. I was still treating it as a physical trip rather than an ethereal one.

In part, I needed to prove to myself that I was capable of this undertaking. I hadn't yet realized my journey would teach me more about surrendering control and embracing what comes our way than how to follow a detailed vacation itinerary. I was not there to see the sights. My destination was inward. I planned what I needed to purchase and the logistics of getting there, but I hadn't yet done much mental preparation.

About a month before I left for Death Valley, I undertook a medicine walk as suggested by Sparrow Hart. This was to be a one-day journey to a destination in the wild. It was like a training session to ensure I was prepared for multiple days of hiking, exposure to the elements, and the physical and mental challenges away from the comforts of home. I chose the top of Angel Island in San Francisco Bay, which is between the city and the south end of Tiburon, California. I had never been to the island, though I'd become familiar with the Bay Area while working at a tech firm in San Jose. I never moved there but commuted twice a month from Toronto. The rolling desert hills, beautiful coastlines, and temperate climate of California are in stark contrast to my home in a northern city surrounded by the Great Lakes and their agricultural flatlands.

I loved the area, particularly a tiny coastal town called Half Moon Bay. Just up the coast, the Moss Beach Distillery offered a magnificent view of the Pacific Ocean. I have happy memories there of ordering a bottle of California chardonnay, sitting underneath a warm wool blanket, and watching the sunset over the ocean while listening to the seals play by the bluffs below.

I took a ferry from Fisherman's Wharf in San Francisco to Sausalito. I wore my hiking gear and day pack, which contained some snacks and my journal. I surveyed the other passengers on the open deck of the ferry. Most were day tourists, dressed in T-shirts and shorts suitable for the warm temperatures of the shore but ill-prepared for the cold winds that blew across the bay. They huddled, sharing warmth and discussing where they would dine in Sausalito or another equally touristy destination. I took notes in my journal and contemplated the hike to the island's peak.

As we disembarked, most passengers headed for the central park and confectionery. I turned in the opposite direction and started the trail hike leading to Mount Livermore. It didn't take too long to summit the peak. I arrived at a lookout station with a grand view of the famous red bridge and the city across the bay.

Like most places with such views, it was crowded with a continual stream of tourists and onlookers. They would linger to view the Golden Gate Bridge and then move off down the trail, exhausted from taking selfies and posting on social media. They were here for the vistas and pictures; I was here to find a vision.

I looked around, stepped over the barrier, and trundled twenty or thirty feet down the hill to find a secluded spot among the sagebrush and trees. I used my jacket as a blanket, kicked off my hiking boots and socks, and watched the ships move back and forth under the bridge. I looked at the bridge spanning the magnificent bay and creating a gateway from California to the open Pacific Ocean. It seemed an appropriate view for one about to set metaphorical sail across an open ocean to a destination unseen over the horizon.

I spent the better part of the day there, contemplating my upcoming spiritual journey. I took notes and thought about what I might encounter in Death Valley. I watched as a spider wound its way through the sagebrush.

According to Navajo legend, the spider wove the web of the universe. The spider totem teaches that power is a matter of self-possession rather than size or physical strength. The spider can weave intricate webs with tremendous strength from wispy threads. It speaks of creating paths to your desired outcomes. But the spider should be respected and used sparingly. Its venom and predatory skills are for limited and intended use, not for waste.

The little spider also reminded me of the Scottish folklore about Robert the Bruce and the spider, a treasure in Scottish households. The story goes that Robert the Bruce, defeated by the invading English and hiding in a cave, watched a wee spider swinging to and fro as it wove its web. Watching the spider inspired Robert not to give up. He went on to conquer the English and drive them from Scotland. Well, for a period, at least. Nonetheless, it is an allegory about resilience and persistence. And about strength, not from physical stature but from inner worth and belief in oneself.

As the spider wove its web, I spun my notes into a letter of intent that captured my reasons for undertaking my quest. I compiled a list of motivations and questions that required answers. This letter was a way of organizing my thoughts. My letter contained questions about the threshold I would explore to expose fears and uncertainties, to uncover obstacles preventing me from adopting a new life, and to discover any blocks I had to letting go of old ways.

Letters of intent contain severances: What parts of my life do I wish to leave behind? What attitudes, habits, or beliefs no longer serve me? They also include incorporations: What do I want to call into my life? What new beliefs or attitudes do I wish to accept? What aspects of a new life call to me?

If the severances and incorporations were the what, I needed to declare the how. How will I take on what I wish to manifest? Who are my allies in this quest? Where are my sources of strength? This outline of intentions helped me recognize both the obstacles and the tools I needed to overcome fear and manifest my desired outcome.

When I finished writing, I packed my things, put on my boots, and hiked back to the harbor to find the evening ferry back to the city.

CHAPTER TWO

Preparing for the Physical
and Spiritual Planes

Kitchener-Waterloo, Ontario, Before

"Where are you traveling?" the store rep asked.

I was in my local adventure store, Sparrow Hart's list in hand. Like all serious backpackers, hikers, and trekkers, I had a truckload of supplies to purchase and depended on the experienced staff to guide me. I wanted authentic gear rather than a knockoff kit sold at Walmart or big-box stores. Those were sufficient for the occasional camper but not for this type of trip. Brands such as the North Face, Columbia, Merrell, Osprey, and others were about to become my supporting actors.

"I'm going hiking in Death Valley," I said. My euphemism hid the true intent of my trip.

"Wow, Death Valley. That's serious, man. You're not going on vacation," he said as he eyed me the same way someone might before sending a loved one off and assuming they would never return.

Death Valley is a place of extremes, bookended by two mountain ranges in the northern Mojave Desert, mainly in Inyo County, California, near the border of Nevada. Contrary to its current arid condition, Death Valley was once an inland lake. The abundance of leftover sodium salts and borax drew miners to the area in the late 1800s and early 1900s.

Named for the grim fate of pioneers seeking a shortcut to California during the winter of 1849–1850, Death Valley is considered the hottest place on earth during the summer. Temperatures can swing from a chilling 13 degrees Fahrenheit (−10 degrees Celsius) to a record high of 134 degrees Fahrenheit (57 degrees Celsius), recorded in July 1913.

I glanced at the employee's name tag—Noah—and admired his appearance. He was tall, lean, and sinewy, with long, messy hair and a deep tan. He carried the badge of his time spent outdoors. He looked natural in his store uniform, which resembled a well-used fishing vest, and hiking boots worn proud over miles of use. I imagined him as a kid in ripped Converse runners and worn jeans, blasting past me on a trail somewhere as I waved, breathless and adorned head to toe in ultralight, water-resistant, name-brand hiking gear. He was the genuine article.

"I will be there for ten days, most of it on my own," my ego said, pushing me with what felt like a chest bump.

"Wow," he repeated, like he was buying time as he assessed my odds of survival. I said nothing as he silently weighed my chances. He cleared his throat and then said, "Okay, man, let's start with boots."

The footwear area had a small arched bridge, like one you would see over a creek, covered in molded terrain that mimicked rocks, logs, and other uneven surfaces. It was an ideal test lab for putting boots through their paces. I settled on a pair of Vasques with good ankle support and light, breathable material.

"So," Noah asked, wrapping up the boots, "do you have to carry all your gear, or will you have a base camp?"

I explained how I'd be in a camp for a few days and then traveling light for solo time.

"Let's get you a backpack, and then we can fill it," he said, winding through the rows of displays toward the back wall, where sleeping bags and backpacks hung.

Again, it was no simple decision: Duration of travel, weight of cargo, height of the hiker, and so on all have an impact on the correct choice. With his help and some strap adjustments, I selected a midsize Osprey backpack with a compartment for a water pouch and ample space for gear.

"I have a list of items my guide suggested I bring," I said, attempting to take control of my shopping spree.

"Of course, man," Noah said and bounced on his toes, ready for whatever I threw at him.

"I need two tarps for shelter and to sleep on, but I was going to get those blue ones from a hardware store."

"You don't want those, man," he said with a smile, his expression a mix of surprise and perhaps well-worn experience. "They are too bulky and heavy."

"Lead on," I muttered, slinging on my new backpack. Noah took me throughout the store, filling it up with ultralightweight tarps, dry sacks (one for my backpack and one for my boots to keep unwanted beasties from taking up residence while I slept), and collapsible walking poles.

With each item I placed in my backpack, the trip became more real.

He held up a compact Jetboil isobutane stove. "It's light-weight and the pot is part of the stove, so you don't need extra gear," my shopping guide explained. "It'll boil a whole pot of coffee in less than a minute." I was sold. I asked about carrying camping fuel on the plane, and he recommended I buy it once I landed in California. Noah guided me in selecting a water bottle, a Benchmade folding knife designed for mountain climbers, socks, a hat, first-aid kits, and other essentials.

I felt a bit like a doomsday prepper, sure of the end times, but I was in awe of my new equipment. My ember slowly flickered, like a parent showing extraordinary patience to a child learning a new task. My ember ignored my materialistic joy, knowing all this would quickly fall by the wayside once I discovered that no ultralightweight, high-tech hiking equipment would lessen the burden of the emotional baggage I would carry into the desert.

"Is there anything else on your list, man?"

"Yes, what about a snakebite kit?" I asked.

He blinked and waited for what seemed too long for a natural pause, then took me over to another aisle nearby. "This is what we have, man, but it won't do you any good if you get bit."

"Well, my guide said I need one," I parried, pulling the small box from its hanger on the display.

"Suit yourself, man."

With the kit in my hand, I said, "I think I'm set."

Noah bounded off toward the cash registers. As we approached, he leaned on the counter and addressed the young girl behind the register. "Ava, this dude is hiking in Death Valley by himself for ten days!"

"Wow, I bet you've trekked all over the world if you can take on Death Valley," she assessed as she unpacked my backpack to scan its contents.

I said nothing.

"Okay, man—good luck out there!" With that, Noah turned

and strode, leaning forward onto his toes, back to the footwear area. The girl behind the counter continued to scan items and place them back in my pack.

I felt like a fraud. Here I was, purchasing the latest and greatest in camping technology to undertake a journey that was really about stripping the psyche back to nothing more than its surroundings, alone in the wild.

I uttered my thanks and stepped out of the store into the parking lot. A gust of wind caught the tag hanging from the shoulder strap of my pack and slapped it firmly across my face. I spat the hard paper tag from my mouth and shook my head like I was evading an annoying insect. It was a humbling gesture that reminded me that, no matter how good, my hiking tech was no match for Mother Nature.

I threw my gear in the back seat of my truck and climbed in behind the wheel. *Who am I kidding?* I thought. I might be ready for the base camp, but my preparations were no match for the time I'd spend alone in the desert.

The solo part of my journey required me to go five days without food. Going without food for that long is an essential part of the process. Fasting is a millennia-long tradition, offering suffering, perseverance, and a metabolic stall that weakens the physical body, allowing the transition into the spiritual plane. Traditionally, Native Americans would also forgo water.

In our case, water was a requirement. I would need to consume about ten liters a day to survive in the desert heat. Our guide had legal complications to contend with, unlike the Native Americans, who didn't have lawyers ready to pounce if a village elder was deemed negligent because a young warrior fell afoul of the desert. He was running a guide business, after all. His program was protected in a cocoon of waivers and other legal tools to ensure I was aware of the risks and took full liability for any unwanted outcomes.

Fasting can cause exhaustion, dizziness, weakness, and potential cognitive confusion. While these effects are tolls to be paid on the spiritual road, they are still something to monitor and consider in regard to activity levels and the impact on thinking and problem-solving. A nutrient-deprived mind can be an unfit guide when traversing hillsides, gauging distance, or making potentially lifesaving decisions. I was to discover this firsthand after three days of abstinence.

Medical references and experienced hikers provided varying ideas about how much water was needed, but they were consistent about one thing: Dehydration can kill. In the absence of clinical measures, urine color is a good indicator. Dark urine is a sure sign of dehydration, while light, straw-like urine indicates appropriate hydration.

The problem with water is its weight. Everything in hiking uses weight as the lowest common denominator. Consuming 4 liters of water a day meant carrying 20 liters of water for five days. Each liter weighs 1 kilogram or 2.2 pounds. So that's 20 kilograms, or nearly 45 pounds, just in fluids! The denominator is the weight, while the numerator is the risk of dehydration. It is a vital equation to get right.

Shelter was another consideration. During the day, temperatures reached 100 degrees Fahrenheit and fell into the low 20s at night. A suitably warm sleeping bag, a ground mattress, and a ground sheet would insulate me from losing vital heat, robbed by the cold ground. A tarp would provide shade in a valley known for its reputation as one of the earth's hottest and most formidable places.

The climate was not the only adversary. The desert was a foreboding landscape in which to dwell. The creatures that walked, slithered, crawled, or burrowed all presented a threat. There were mountain lions, bobcats, coyotes, rattlesnakes, and scorpions.

Rattlesnake venom is fast acting and can disable and kill

an adult without timely medical attention, which would not be an option. After walking miles out of the desert from my solo campsite, I would have to drive over two hours back to civilization. Cellular coverage was spotty, making it equally tricky to call medical support, such as a rapid-response helicopter. If I became debilitated, it might take up to twenty-four hours for someone in my group to suspect something was wrong.

"Bite kits are useless for rattlers," Sparrow Hart would later explain. "Attempting to pump out or suck the venom from the wound might look good in cowboy movies, but that only increases the likelihood of ingestion and rapid metabolization." This, even though he'd included it on my supply list. More legal loopholes.

Placing a tourniquet on a bitten limb could cause additional complications. "If you get bitten, lie down and get ready for the worst two days of your life," Sparrow Hart warned. Remaining still would help slow the spread of the venom, and then you just hope for the best and pray for help to arrive.

Scorpion stings are less lethal but extremely painful. The stung area will swell and turn black, and the sting of the Arizona bark scorpion is excruciating, leading some victims to beg for an amputation. A sting in a backyard, with medical assistance nearby, is one thing. But a quick path to suffering in the middle of Death Valley is another.

Tarantulas were present but less concerning. These nocturnal creatures were more of a nuisance than a threat. If handled or startled, they can release irritating hairs, especially aggravating if they become lodged in the eyes. However, even if they bite, the sensation is more akin to a bee sting—temporary and less painful.

It was not only animals that represented a threat. Plants were as aggressive and nasty as their animal counterparts. Various species of cacti could cause pain and infection. Jumping cholla, for instance, grows detachable thorns. Of course, the barbs do not jump, but they latch on and break away from the mother plant. They are challenging (and painful) to remove. Simply brushing the plant can lead to stinging scratches and secondary infection.

I imagined lying in agony as snake venom circulated through my body. The impending stabs of pain, cramping, fever, and hallucinations would be my only company as I lay waiting for someone to discover me. How long would I lie there? Or would a mountain lion or other predator be the first to arrive on the scene?

How could I know that the physical threats and risks were the only ones I could foresee and mitigate? What I could not predict were the spiritual pitfalls. For those, I had no way of preparing. My adventure store didn't sell a spirit-bite kit.

—

A spiritual wilderness journey occurs on two planes: the physical and the spiritual. The physical plane involves staying hydrated, understanding the side effects of fasting, being aware of the local plants and animals, selecting appropriate clothing and equipment, and knowing emergency procedures. I'd prepared for all that as much as I could.

The spiritual plane, on the other hand, is embodied in rituals and ceremonies that transition from the physical to meet the sacred. It's in the spiritual realm that we communicate and connect. This was the reason I was going, and besides my letter of intent, I hadn't spent much time considering what this would be like.

In the final weeks before the vision quest, Sparrow Hart instructed me to form a council of allies. In the absence of traditional tribal elders, I would select a small group of people to assist me in making final preparations for my quest. Traditionally, allies could include other tribal members or colleagues with similar roles who could help the traveler gather what they needed, find strength, or provide emotional support. I chose five people.

The first was a coworker with whom I was close. Kathy was about my age and held a similar professional rank. We met at RIM, the company that developed BlackBerry mobile devices with a keyboard. It was a heady time in technology, and the company lacked the prerequisite experience to be the billion-dollar business it was. Chaos, politics, and fratricide were the norm. Those of us who had worked in more mature organizations knew this was a recipe for disaster and foretold a rather grim fall for the firm.

Colleagues either became comrades or enemies as they faced off across a boardroom table that served as our Maginot Line. Emails flew back and forth like bombs and mortars. Having someone to trust was critical to survival in such a combative climate, and Kathy was that lifeline for me. She seemed like someone who could be my ally in this new conflict. When I asked her, she was curious but instantly willing to help.

"That is groovy as shit, Markie-Mark," she said, using her nickname for me, after I explained the trip. "Just don't get killed, you idiot."

"I will do my best, K."

My second ally was Archie, a transplanted Brit whom I'd met while working in a different start-up technology firm. He was born in North London but had followed employment opportunities across the US and Canada, a true nomad. He'd transferred in from another company in Montreal, Quebec. He was living alone in a dungeon-like basement apartment until he could find a house and move his family to Waterloo, Ontario.

While the English and Scots do not always see eye to eye, my Canadian upbringing tempered any prescribed cultural disdain for his English heritage. I felt bad for him living alone in a damp room, so I often invited him to dinner with my family and to hang out on weekends. Over the months, we became close friends. He felt like a brother.

His English genes granted him a slick talent at soccer—or football, as he rightly called it. He was agile for his tall height and could move smoothly through defenders with the ball no more than a step from his feet. The ball seemed glued to his body, as if held by an invisible force. I was a solid backline defender, though nowhere near his level of talent. He was a striker who could make or break a team. I envied his skills.

Here, I had the leg up. Spirituality, or any subject beyond engineering and the science of touch and feel, was beyond his grasp. Despite not being spiritual, he appreciated that I was seeking answers in a language he did not understand. During my weeks of contemplation, he was aware of my growing interest in going on this spiritual journey in the wilderness. He gravitated to the nature-survival aspects of my trip.

"Look, mate, I don't understand what you are looking for, but I can see you are in pain," he rationalized. "I've got your back." He was in.

My third council member was much different from the first two. Edwin was the founder of the cybersecurity firm where I worked. He was a Renaissance man, a technology authority who had built an enviable reputation in the hedge funds on Wall Street. He was also an expert in martial arts. His office was a cramped, eclectic mix of computer parts and Buddhist knickknacks, adorned with conference badges hung from various lamps and stands around the room. It was a bit like Mulder's basement office in *The X-Files*.

The company could have been a fraternity house for the lack of women and overabundance of middle-aged white men. Of the people there, Edwin seemed to recognize something beyond cold business objectives. He had a chivalry to him. He'd spent enough time on Wall Street to realize the "bright lights, big city" mindset ended in addiction, rehab, and lone-liness. Valuing his family over his career, he came back to the Waterloo region, leaving the glare of Wall Street behind. He was the only colleague who appreciated my endeavor.

When I asked him to join my council, he responded in his usual way. His lips were held tight as he nodded his head up and down, yielding a stoic "Yeah, yeah, of course."

He stood up from behind his cluttered desk and leaned forward, his hand outstretched to shake mine. He held a slight bow and placed his left hand under his right wrist, waiting to shake my hand. He looked me in the eye and bowed his head. "Thank you."

Michelle was my fourth member. We met in 2013, in the spring after my father's passing. She was a consultant at my company, an expert in navigating personality, building high-functioning executive teams, and helping businesses through restructuring. When we first met, I was impatient and rude because she'd been late. It turned out she'd been waiting in the office lobby and could not get in. It didn't take long for her to see through my gruff exterior to expose the wounded person desperate for someone to see them and understand who they truly were.

After her contract was complete, we stayed in touch. She emanated a light unlike that of other people I had met. She was to the point and relished calling out people's bullshit, including mine. She was more than a professional sage; she was groovy. Also a practitioner and certified yoga instructor, Michelle was well-versed in the properties of crystals, a tarot reader, and a believer in an all-connected universe. Her language of spiritual practice was Wiccan rather than Native American, but it was still something we had in common.

We had lunch one workday, and I asked her to join my council. She was eager to hear the details, and I explained the process I'd been working through.

"Part of my preparations requires that I form a council of allies." I went on to explain the details and member obligations.

"Are you asking me to be on your council?" she asked.

"I am," I responded. "You're a good friend and have always given me good advice, even if I didn't want it." I smirked.

"Fuck yeah, I will!" She whooped. "Mark, I am so proud of you for facing your demons." Even though I knew she would accept, I felt a sense of relief. I needed to know she was in my corner.

"You can't look after yourself," Michelle joked. "You need someone like me to save your ass."

My last council member was the most important—my daughter. She would be my tether to this life. Simultaneously, she was my reason to venture into the desert and my reason to return. Of course, Rebecca was too young to serve on a formal council. She was six at the time, too young to fully comprehend what I was about to do. Yet she had everything I needed in an anchor.

One week before my scheduled departure, my council of allies gathered in a crowded sushi restaurant. Individually, each member had a strength I needed. Together, we were an awkward bunch of strangers who had nothing in common, except me and my aspirations of teasing death in the desert. They introduced themselves, then settled into silence.

"Thank you for joining me," I opened. "I know this is unusual. I appreciate your support." Edwin bowed his head, and Kathy took a sip of her drink. Archie was out of his depth, and Michelle sat with her hands linked. She was beaming.

"I will start by reading my letter of intent," I announced, unfolding the clean papers on which my letter was printed. In response, the men sat silently, likely desperate to eat. The women expounded on their interpretations of my intentions. In turn, I expressed their importance to me, then asked them to hold vigil.

"Each night, I ask you to light a candle and say a prayer for my safety, and to call Spirit to my aid." Kathy and Michelle smiled, confirming their intent to honor my request.

"Sure," Archie said, and Edwin nodded in affirmation. I was confident that Edwin and Archie never intended to honor my request. This woo-woo stuff was a step too far for them.

"I got you something," Michelle said. She pulled a small envelope of tan tissue paper from her bag and handed it to me.

I unfolded the tissues to reveal a small purse on a leather string.

"It's a deer-hide medicine bag," she said. "You wear it around your neck."

Indigenous peoples of the Americas traditionally wore medicine bags filled with sacred items, perhaps symbols of their journey, lessons, or markers of their tribe.

"Thank you, Michelle." I was moved. It was lovely.

We finished our meal, and each person departed. Edwin made excuses about an impending call and left. Karen stood and gave me a bear hug. "Be safe," she said, then turned and bounded from the restaurant.

Michelle and I lingered, slowly making our way to the door. Once we were outside, we hugged. She whispered, "You got this." She turned and walked across the parking lot toward her car. The light and color of my life seem to follow her, leaving me alone in a grayed-out, hueless world. It seemed I was already in the desert, even before I set foot on the airplane to Death Valley.

—

Rebecca and I had started a little ritual to lessen the lost time when I constantly traveled for work. I bought a small plush dragon, which she pragmatically named Dragon. This six-inch purple toy would accompany me on all my trips. Dragon would take selfies wherever we traveled and text them home so Rebecca could see. It was a means to remain connected and to make my travel relatable to her. But this trip would be different.

"Hey, DD," I called, using Rebecca's reserved nickname. When she was little, she could not say "baby" correctly when referring to her dolls. They were her "DDs." I started calling her by this nickname, which she accepted. When other people tried to use this moniker, she would wrinkle her nose indignantly. "Only Daddy can call me that!" she declared, crossing her arms. "I'm Rebecca to you."

She was sitting on the couch in the living room, her eyes glued to the television.

"Yeah?" she responded without looking away from the latest Disney princess movie.

"You know Daddy is going on his special trip tomorrow," I continued.

"Yeah," she acknowledged without breaking her gaze.

"Well, you know how I always take Dragon on trips." I spoke to the side of her head. "Well, Dragon can't come on this one."

"Okay," she said, unfazed and too distracted to care.

I soldiered on. "Since this trip is special, I got *you* something instead."

"What is it?" she inquired, still focused on Disney.

"I got you a magical cheetah," I said, producing a wooden totem and placing it into her visual path, breaking her trance. It was a simple wooden cylinder painted with the cheetah's distinctive spots and a carved feline head adorned with the recognizable nose stripes and tawny neck. It was small enough to fit in her hand, so she could keep it with her wherever she went.

Cheetahs were Rebecca's favorite animal. She loved their grunts and the way cubs yipped and chirped to call their mother. She loved watching wilderness shows and could rhyme off details about the big African cats.

"Wow!" she said, taking the totem and shifting it in her hand to explore its surface and inspect the details. "What's the magic, Daddy?"

"Well, when you talk to the cheetah, she can come and tell me what you said."

She stared at me with skepticism. "That's not possible. You said you're going far away."

"I did," I responded. "But this cheetah is magical and runs fast. So fast she can come to me and then run back to you without you even noticing she was gone."

"Wow! That *is* magical," she said excitedly. I finally had her full attention. She turned the cheetah totem over again as if trying to locate the source of the magic.

I sat beside her to watch her program. After a long pause, she turned and threw her arms around me, burying herself in my chest. "I will miss you, Daddy."

"I will miss you, too, DD."

In that glimmer of a moment, I had all the resilience and strength I needed to find my answers in the sands of Death Valley and return to my anchor.

CHAPTER THREE

Leaving the World I Knew

Big Cedar, California, Days 0–3

I set out among the other travelers from Toronto boarding a flight to Las Vegas. I stowed my basic supplies in my backpack, wore my bulky hiking boots, which took up too much space in my luggage, and checked the rest in a big purple suitcase. As I slid into my seat on the plane, I realized my hiking clothes did not match the garb of my fellow travelers. I felt a vibration, perhaps the glow of my inner ember urging me on, among a crowd donned in shorts and flip-flops, anticipating the allure of the Strip's gambling venues and stage shows.

I'd been to Las Vegas many times before, all for business. It was a plastic model of the real world, an adult playground for people who liked immediate gratification and did not care if it was the real thing or not—fake castles, fake pirates, fake Egyptian pyramids, fake Venetian canals, and so on. Lacking any authenticity, it had plenty of room for visitors' secrets.

Las Vegas was also a mirror held up to society, reflecting a dwindling stack of chips, which made me think we were one lousy hand from bust. I collected my luggage and picked up my rental car, a basic compact SUV capable of taking me from the Neon City to a valley lit by the stars. The incessant chimes of slot machines gave way to the sound of my tires on the black-top. I welcomed the change to my soundtrack.

I drove north up Interstate 95, passing through Red Canyon National Park, and then headed toward Beatty, Nevada. The interstate met a small highway, where oversize gas stations and rest stops greeted weary travelers. The farther north I traveled, the more the landscape became rugged; towns resembled a mix of something out of a cowboy movie and a junkyard filled with all that America had built and then tossed aside like un-wanted toys. Broken appliances, worn furniture, and vehicle carcasses littered the yards. The locals were as weathered as their chosen place of residence. Their gaze was somewhere be-tween welcoming to strangers and resentful of their reliance on a conveyor belt of strangers for their income.

I fueled up, grabbed a snack, and kept going. Civilization faded, replaced by signs that warned No GAS FOR 90 MILES. The interstate narrowed to one lane, as if rationing its asphalt to make the journey through desolation to the next rest stop. Cars became fewer. And the ones that did pass had seen their share of miles: sagging suspension, blemishes of rust, and mis-matched tires.

Somewhere near the Timbisha Reservation, I stopped at a store, no more than a shack. It was once a gas station, but a lack of local traffic had withered it to a small convenience stop. Inside, I purchased a rusty-orange wool blanket. I did not need it, but I felt I should make some offering to the wrinkled relic of a woman working there. I traded seven bucks for the blanket and kept driving. No words passed between us.

After hours of monotony, I turned west onto Highway 266 toward the state border. The arid landscape gave way to scrub cattle pastures. Somewhere past Magruder Mountain and Last Chance Mountain, I crossed into California and took Highway 168 at Oasis over the White Mountains through Westgard Pass toward Big Pine. The mountains refused an easy path, forcing the road to slither like a snake through the hills. Finally, the winding and twisting of the road settled into a consistent descent, and I broke through the mountain pass into the valley and drove into Big Pine, a small town of no more than two thousand people. I continued past signs for the hot springs to Baker Creek Campground, where I was to meet up with fellow travelers and our guide the following day.

I stayed in my car the first night, too excited to sleep. I was overwhelmed by the beauty of the Sierra Nevada, which stood vigil over the town. The mountains could perform magic, transmuting from gray, snowcapped giants to fiery-pink flamingos at sunrise. They announced the new day, plumping their snowy plumage to reflect the rising sun. They rivaled the Grand Canyon in their way, and they were capable of chameleonlike color changes.

I awoke to the mountain's morning display, truly appreciating that the desert was not a dull, monotonous tan. That was the canvas. The sky, mountains, and streams could produce an array of turquoise and cobalt blues, pinks and bloodreds, and lush greens, defiant of their monotone surroundings.

Later in the morning, I met up with Sparrow Hart and the rest of the group.

"You made it from Canada," Sparrow Hart said, shaking my hand as he surveyed the preparations underway.

Others arrived over the next hour. Nancy was our oldest member, a retired nurse from the Midwest. Sam had retired from investment banking on the East Coast. Glen was a retired techie who drove in from the Bay Area in California. Kevin, a fellow Canadian, had driven from Kingston, Ontario, nearly 2,400 miles (4,000 kilometers) to join our quest. He was a professor at his local university. Ophelia was our youngest member. She was shy about her background, and we did not pry.

In a day, we would all share our deepest secrets, revealing more to this small group of strangers than any of us had told our closest kin. That first day, we were shy and awkwardly polite as we found our place to camp among the trees. We would be there for a few days before adjourning for our solo time. We would then return for two days to regroup, share our tales, and offer interpretations and lessons.

We ventured back to Bishop, where an adventure-supply store sold cooking gas and freeze-dried meals. There was also a Starbucks, where I used the Wi-Fi to connect with people back home.

I was excited to be in the midst of an adventure. I was painfully aware that the people I'd left behind were scared. I knew some, like my wife, were less concerned about the physical risk of solo desert travel than what this trip represented in terms of my future intentions. Would I be coming home? If so, would I be the same person who left? What was I truly seeking? What would I find? How would my life change? And would they be a part of the new version of me?

I set my camp beside the burbling Baker Creek, where the air was at least ten degrees colder. The creek carried the meltwater from the snow-covered Sierra Nevada caps and chilled everything around it. I pitched my yellow coffin tent and strung my hammock between two trees. The first night, I ditched the claustrophobic tent for my hammock. With nothing but air underneath me, I was colder than I would've been in the tent. I burrowed into my sleeping bag and wrapped the rust-orange blanket around me for extra insulation. I gave a silent prayer of thanks to the elderly Indigenous woman who'd sold it to me.

The sounds of the creek lulled me to sleep, only to be woken by a blue heron boldly raiding my bag of food hanging from a branch nearby. According to some Indigenous traditions, the heron conveys self-determination and self-reliance. Other coastal nations believe the heron symbolizes patience and good luck. I would need the luck. It could keep my breakfast.

Across the creek lay a ragged hill, which I climbed each morning at the group camp to meditate and practice yoga as the sun rose, painting the mountains around me. From there, I could see the world. My world, at least. It was at once clean air and breathtaking vistas. I felt safe on my outcrop. At the top, I built an eagle-shaped cairn as an offering. I asked Eagle to share her vision and help me see Spirit. It became my daily ceremony—a physical manifestation of my desire to connect with Source.

Later that day, Sparrow Hart gathered our group together. We sat in a circle and watched as he opened his old robin's-egg-blue backpack and pulled out a leather pouch. From the pouch, he removed an abalone shell, a palm-size mollusk bowl with a pearly sheen on the interior. He then removed a small bag of what turned out to be crushed sage. He poured a small measure of sage into the abalone and then used a match to light the sage. He blew on the pile until it smoldered, and eddies of smoke wafted from the shell. Once he was satisfied with the volume of smoke emanating from the shell, he stood.

"This is called smudging," Sparrow Hart explained. We watched in silence as he wafted the bowl and its smoke around his body. "The smoke cleanses. Sage is used to remove bad energy." Once he had moved the bowl around his head, he asked, "Who would like to go next?"

"I will," Ophelia said, standing to take the bowl from his outstretched hands. He watched as she repeated the same process of smudging. We each took turns. I felt awkward smudging, but my inner ember glowed with encouragement. Kevin, the last to go, passed the shell back to Sparrow Hart, who placed it down in front of him.

"In our first group session, we will explore the elements of a vision quest," announced Sparrow Hart.

We sat in a loose circle, cross-legged in the scrub grass with our notebooks, and watched as he reached into his weathered blue backpack and pulled out his own ragged notebook. His pack resembled something a child would use to carry books to and from school. But its faded and frayed appearance proved that it could withstand its owner's travels through barren and hostile environments. He searched a pocket in his cargo pants and found his pen.

"The first is fasting," he said. "The lack of food slows the metabolism as the body begins to eat its fat reserves and stimulates a change of consciousness," he explained. I intellectualized his words, but that was far different from experiencing the shift from the physical to the spiritual plane.

Solitude, the second element, removes the traveler from their known world and strips them of routine. It creates a space, or silence, for visions, messages, or other forms of communication. A connection to nature is critical. To get closer to Source, the traveler must return to the wild and shed the safety of the familiar. This element requires the traveler to leave their home and community to live among the animals, with the ground for their bed and the stars for their shelter.

The last element is the duration. "Typically, the traveler will spend three days preparing, five days of fasting in solitude, and two days in the community to integrate," he explained. This elixir of elements leads the traveler to understand their path in life, serving as a medicine to anchor them to their purpose.

Over the next few days, we studied the medicine wheel

and its four shields. And we learned about ritual and ceremony. The medicine wheel, also called the sacred hoop, illustrated by a circle equally divided into four colored sections, represents the Great Everything—the circle of life, as the Lakota call it. The sections represent the four winds, or shields. Each shield represents a cardinal direction, starting and finishing in the east (east, south, west, north, and back to east). They each also represent a season (spring, summer, autumn, and winter), a cosmic state of being (spirit, soul, body, mind), and a milestone of maturity (childhood, adolescence, adulthood, and old age).

These shields are usually associated with an animal totem, which varies across Indigenous communities, depending on the local species. These animals symbolize the purpose of each shield.

An example medicine wheel illustrating the Lakota (Sioux) shield animals.

The four shields are perfectly symmetrical, symbolizing how no one shield is more important than another. Nor is any one shield closer to Source. Each is a crucial stage of life, whether it refers to a person's lifetime, the seasonality of nature, or our perception of existence and participation in society.

Sparrow Hart guided us through prequest meditation to

help us determine which shield (direction) we were stuck in. Someone who is trapped at a particular maturity stage often feels drawn to a specific shield. A childhood memory or wound might throb as they meditate on the four shields. My letter of intent outlined my observations. I knew that to continue my journey through the sacred hoop, I had to find the strength of the south and face the shadows of my adolescence.

The south should be a time of highlights. It's noon and the summer. It is the time of the Soul and a time of adolescence. The first lesson the south teaches us is trust. As children, we acquire confidence (trust) from those around us. Our families feed and shelter us, and our communities support our growth. A child who is not protected will never learn to trust and will be wary of loved ones or fear—and even expect—betrayal.

The second lesson is innocence. Trust is the world, and innocence is the self. While complementary, innocence is the expression and emotion of the self. A well-functioning south shield produces a zest for life and a zeal for expression. A person must trust those around them to express their true selves. An out-of-balance south shield can manifest as an obsession with wealth, material things, and selfishness. And that was me. I was desperate for the approval of others.

Indigenous cultures were originally highly integrated societies that depended on each villager to support the collective. Elders interpreted the young traveler's dreams or visions, sometimes of animals (totems), to determine the adolescent's path. Guided by these visions, the young person would become a student or apprentice of an adult in their role. These quests had a holistic purpose, with a specific function necessary to the tribe's well-being.

As my pen scribbled across the pages of my leather journal, I pondered the notion of purpose, which I often intertwined with pragmatism. I and my fellow members of Generation X were told to get "real" jobs, namely those endorsed by society and that would provide for a nuclear family. By definition, arts and drama—the fundamentals of creativity—were somehow less important than plumbing and farming. "Work hard and be rewarded" was the promise of my parents' generation, and they'd passed those beliefs on to us. But now, we had so much personal, spiritual unrest. We weren't living our true purposes.

That was where this esoteric form of spiritual journeying came in.

Non-Native observers and anthropologists believe that traditional elements of the vision quest, such as fasting and solitude, lead to a comatose state, perhaps tapping into the subconscious to reveal a desired course in life. Spiritual journeys can also help address other mental and emotional blockages. Often, people seek healing from deep trauma or emotional injury. People who have experienced unstable or violent childhood homes or those who are victims of sexual abuse or violent relationships look to heal from such trauma. A close friend of mine revealed sexual abuse at the hands of his family doctor. His parents not only ignored their child's cry for help but also punished him for fabricating stories. They later discovered that their child was not the only victim of this predator. As part of his healing process, he chose the medicine of Indigenous groups in South America, through ayahuasca journeying.

While this has been criticized as appropriating Indigenous tradition, many people who go on quests seeking spiritual medicine for a disorder or injury, myself included, intend only to honor this ceremony. I wasn't partaking in a vision quest for profit, at least not in economic terms. I hoped to learn and grow personally. I expected to heal my wounds. It was medicine to me. It was therapy in a language that resonated with my soul.

I could have relied solely on brain chemistry–altering

pharmaceuticals to dull my pain and attended weekly therapy sessions to process my emotional sins. To me, this industrialized approach to mental health was a perpetual machine designed to treat symptoms. Facing myself in the desert was a full-frontal charge toward what hurt me. I was partaking in a medicine shared through Indigenous tradition with only the greatest reverence and honor for the culture.

After lunch, it was our turn to lead the conversation. We shared our stories and our aspirations for the journey. Some of my fellow travelers were lost, looking for purpose again. They were the grist cast aside by corporate grinders. Years of service and expertise were shed like skin as the profit serpent grew and fed on its employees. These shadows sought a new beginning. It was more than sourcing an income. They needed a connection to a group—something larger than themselves. Some, especially those fresh to retirement, felt they had been banished from the group where they'd belonged for so many years. They were lost in the urban wilderness. They had a purpose and could grow corn, but no one was there to receive their gifts. Some sought atonement for perceived sins. They had been calloused, obedient servants feeding the bulldozer that spared little in the search for investor profits. Their prosperity was traded for moral bankruptcy, from which they sought escape. Perhaps you have to attain everything to realize you have nothing.

One traveler was a retired investment banker. He had spent his life taking and giving little in return. And he knew it. He sought forgiveness. He sought a connection to something more than steel-and-glass towers. He was atoning for his self-recognized sins.

Another had undertaken several quests, each a step closer to easing their conscience after a career of helping corporations bulldoze workers, competitors, and the environment. They knew their sins and dedicated the remainder of their life to making amends. Their guilty plea to economic crimes was ironic proof of their residual humanity.

Others were the casualties of our disconnected society. Their innocence was robbed one domestic-abuse punch at a time, stolen by power brokers in white coats and community leaders wearing vestments, or taken silently through sexual abuse. They had been ignored by the families that should have protected them and left behind by broken community safeguards that should have prevented such shameful crimes. A year before we arrived in Big Pine, one traveler had cycled from Florida to California, towing his physically impaired partner in a bicycle trailer. They had planned for years to make the trip together when they retired. Before they could, his partner was diagnosed with multiple sclerosis. He was too debilitated to participate physically. So this man cycled them both from one coast to the other, cutting a path across the United States. Now he was here in Big Pine, heading into the desert. Their stories were inspiring and heart wrenching.

I did not measure up to the loss of some of my fellow travelers. At times, I felt like a tourist, making this trip simply to prove I could rather than because I had no other choice. I was seeking to expand, looking for a path forward. These people were desperate to rebuild from their ashes. I didn't yet understand about the demon of comparison and how we are each on our own path.

On the last night in Big Pine, I purchased some firewood, and we danced and sang around the fire. One of our party members strummed his guitar and performed a song he had written but had never sung publicly before. His music was reminiscent of Harry Chapin's melodies, paired with the profound lyrics of Eddie Vedder. It brought tears to my eyes with a tenderness and awareness that made me want to avoid ever stepping on a blade of grass lest I hurt it. His gentleness was a reminder to be kind to all living beings.

—

The following morning, I meditated on my hilltop, then packed up, and our caravan headed south. After a two-hour drive, I stepped out of the car and into Death Valley. My boots landed in the soft dust. Like Armstrong landing on the moon, I took one small step for man and one giant leap for myself. For miles around, the valley appeared to be a dry lake bed. In each direction were mountains. Nature held dominion. I checked my phone to confirm what I knew: There was no signal in this foreboding place. I said a small prayer for those who had traversed this way and never made it out.

We spent the rest of the day preparing for our solo time. First, we discussed the shield we wished to explore. This would help determine which direction to take from here. I chose south, still focused on my need to heal my inner child who couldn't trust. Another traveler, Sam, decided the same direction. He had the look of a marathon runner, sinewy and made for long durations of travel. I was glad to know he would be the closest person to me. If I got in trouble, he could carry me out.

The next step was finding a suitable location for my five-day solitude. This involved hiking out into the valley three times, like Everest climbers moving up and down between camps to acclimatize to the altitude. Similarly, my first trip was to establish my solo base camp, somewhere far enough to find isolation yet close enough to walk back from, after being beleaguered and starved for five days.

Once I found a suitable location, I would return to our base of operations to collect my water supply and then take it back to the determined solo-camp location. There, I would store it somewhere safe before returning to the base of operations again. The third trip would mark the beginning of my solo wilderness quest, the push to the summit.

On my first hike out into the valley, I discovered that the

flat-looking desert terrain was anything but flat. Washouts
blocked my path every few hundred feet. Desiccated scrub lay
strewn on a canvas of sand, pebbles, and rocks. The landscape
was almost alien and devoid of obvious life. The sand was like
a thin, dry crust, spotted with small pinprick holes. My cadence was disrupted every time I stepped on a hidden burrow
beneath the surface and it collapsed, sinking my foot into the
ground up to my ankle. It was like walking across a partially
frozen puddle. At times, the glass-like surface is strong enough
to support a walker, and at others, the fragile surface cracks
and sinks into the cold water below.

The washouts were the sketches of nature that proved the
eternal battle between water and the arid landscape was real.
Some washouts were inches deep, capillaries that led to canyons cut six feet deep in the ground. Others were dried-out
arteries. These trenches were cut by flooding water that raged
from the surrounding mountains, bathing the planes with its
life-giving essence. Deep washouts were strewn with rocks
and smoothed pieces of bleached wood, washed down from
the surrounding mountains. Their sides crumbled as you tried
to climb, but the floors were hard and compact.

There was no way to establish a rhythm. Trekking was
slow going and required constant attention to my footing. I
approached a dark, rocky butte, which seemed appropriate for
reaching Spirit. I made a trail up the hillside between boulders, giving room around sagebrush, which likely served as the
home of scorpions. I wore leather gloves to avoid cuts from
sharp stones or bites from the creatures I feared.

Bands of sand wound between the rocks and boulders.
Sizable chunks of rose quartz lay freely in the sand. It was a
bounty of crystals that people might treasure from a shop in
town. They were there for the taking, but part of our quest was
a promise to leave everything as we found it and take nothing out.

As I climbed the hill, I made small cairns to guide me back. When I reached the top, I found a slight depression among several large rocks guarding the drop-off to the valley floor below. This was the place. I would find my purpose here as I took in the view of the valley. My scouting mission was complete. I had found my place in the physical plane. I returned to our base camp in the valley below to continue with preparations.

By late afternoon, I sat with my fellow travelers, quietly talking. This was our trench in the war. Tomorrow, we'd push over the top into the waiting clutches of the wild and into whatever our journey would show us. We were nervous, scared even, and doing our best to pretend the morning would not come.

I spent some time chatting with my fellow Canadian, Kevin, the person who had driven from Ontario to California, taking over a month to make the journey. He was a university professor, and the bond formed was over more than our mutual citizenship. We thought alike and overintellectualized our quest. We spent the time pondering a future business that could offer a watered-down version of this kind of journey to people not ready to face themselves in isolation. In hindsight, this was appropriation, best left unfulfilled. It was a spur-of-the-moment idea, more mature than our days-long acquaintance. It was more than a distraction, but less than a commitment to each other.

The air was chilly as we staked down our ground sheets and prepared to sleep with no ceiling to protect us. From the air, we must have looked like a line of corpses brought off the battlefield, waiting to be shipped home in boxes. I lay there, making a silent bargain with "that which crawled and slithered" to avoid finding an unwanted companion in my sleeping bag. It was the first real night of desert camping. Tomorrow, we would step out of our medicine circle and go our separate ways to find what awaited us.

I lay on the ground, trying to sleep. I stared at the stars that formed words across a celestial book's page in my mind. I would tell the tale of a warrior returning from the desert to lead his people. I would tell the story of the wilderness quest and the conquest of powerful existential fear. I thought again of Chris McCandless.

After graduating from Emory University, McCandless drove from Virginia to Lake Mead in California. Before he left, he donated his money, burned his ID, and removed the license plates from his old Datsun. After he disavowed himself from society and escaped the pain of his troubled family, he assumed the pseudonym Alexander Supertramp.

Under this name, he traveled from Mexico to Alaska, where he entered the bush. He found an old school bus converted into a hunting lodge (which he named the Magic Bus) and lived off the land. Months later, hunters stumbled upon the bus and discovered his decomposing body. The last coherent entry in his journal implied that he ate berries, which led some to speculate that he died of poisoning.

Let's be clear, I do not romanticize his death. After all, his journey was about living, truly living, instead of just surviving in a society he considered hypocritical and oppressive. To me, Chris McCandless wanted to find his authenticity by returning to nature. I believe that McCandless had every intention of returning to his societal life once his alter ego, Alexander Supertramp, found peace in the wild. It is tragic that a simple accident led to his death, but nature is not forgiving.

I had not given away my possessions, burned my ID, or disappeared. Unlike Chris, I was coming back. I was the low-commitment version of a vagabond. I was Alex Ordinary Tramp, and there would be no Eddie Vedder guitar riffs or introspective lyrics layered behind my form as I trudged across the desert vista.

PART TWO

Initiation

CHAPTER FOUR

Smashing Illusions

Death Valley, California, Days 4–5

By morning, I was no longer the hero of my story but a scared soldier praying to survive the impending battle. My bravery had awakened early and deserted me. Abandoned, I was relegated to pathetic bargaining with the ethereal. Why had I decided on this dangerous seclusion in a natural prison that killed its inhabitants? That morning, I felt I would accept a watered-down Las Vegas version of Death Valley—flora and fauna mimicked by hyperlifelike decorations, drinks served regularly, and a concierge there to help me if I couldn't find my way to the pool.

I packed away my sleeping gear and prepared my pack for the journey ahead. The others did likewise. No one spoke. We were already shifting to a solitary mindset, even though we kept physical company. It was time to depart for our solo time.

Nearby, Sparrow Hart was preparing a medicine circle. On the ground, he placed rocks at the cardinal directions and enough stones to outline a ring, then entered from the east. "Please join me," he directed. We formed around the circumference and stood facing one another, Sparrow Hart at the center. He opened our safe space, giving thanks to the four winds and asking their respective totems to share their medicine.

"When you are ready," Sparrow Hart began, "please step forward in front of me." His voice was quiet yet unwavering. He was a paradoxical cornerstone in our ceremonial circle. He was patient as we stood still. "Take your time. There is no rush to get where you are going." This was the gangplank to our voyage.

—

After what seemed like hours, one of the women in our group stepped into the circle. She removed her sun hat and stood silently. Sparrow Hart wafted a red-tailed hawk feather to distribute eddies of sage smoke burning from his abalone shell. He bathed her heart, head, and limbs in the sage smoke and called in the spirits to guide her.

"I ask Bear to share her strength with you, to bless you with courage, and to protect you in your solitude," he said. Tears slowly ran down her cheeks, and she sniffed to pull back the snot and control her fear.

"Go when you are ready," he gently urged her.

Sparrow Hart was no longer the guide. It was as if the ritual had opened an unseen door, and it was her job to step through and find what lay invisible on the other side. She was crying, her tears in stark contrast to our thirsty valley. She sniffed loudly, wiped the tears from her cheeks, and whimpered, "It's time." With that, she stepped out and headed west. Within minutes, she was a diminishing iota set against the desert.

I looked down at my boots. I took my brimmed hat from my head and stepped before our elder. Like he had with others before me, Sparrow Hart smudged to cleanse me and addressed the spirits. "Wolf, we ask that you lend your intuition and instincts to help Mark see his path."

I could no longer meet his eyes. I knew he had seen that look in so many other travelers before they departed from a similar ceremony. I put my hat on to hide the tears welling in my eyes and thanked my scarf for hiding the lump in my throat. I kept my head down as I marched south to find myself. My walking poles dug small rings in the sand, and my boots kicked up wakes of dust as I trod across the baked ground.

I headed south for my dark butte, my fear distracted by the necessity of carefully placing every step. It took the better part of an hour to return to the dry riverbed that was the home to the stone pile I shared with my fellow south traveler, Sam. Over millennia, travelers developed a clever means by which they could signal "everything is okay" without breaking their solitude: a simple stone pile.

Together, Sam and I built an obvious stone pile in an agreed-upon and mutually attainable location (about a mile from our separate camp locations). In the morning, Sam would place the capstone on the ground in front of the pile. Then, in the afternoon, I would return and replace the capstone atop the cairn. In this way, we would each know the other was safe. If either of us returned and discovered the stone in the wrong place, we were to assume our partner was in distress and head back out of the desert to an assigned meeting place to seek help.

It was still intact, the capstone at its zenith. I continued toward the onyx butte, becoming more comfortable with my surroundings. The morning was warm. I stopped to shed my orange anorak and push my sweater sleeves up. I kept my hat and scarf on to protect my head and neck from the sun.

When I reached the foot of the butte, I began climbing the sandy waterfall that rode the rocks above down to the flat plain of the valley. I climbed up the slow grade, looking for the cairns I had built to guide the way. The darker black rocks and pinkish quartz crystals contrasted with the almost colorless sand.

I was well up the black mass when I spotted one of my cairns. I was on the right track. I shifted my pack to relieve the growing ache in my shoulder and kept hiking upward. Twenty minutes later, I reached the top and found my hovel.

For the rest of the morning, I settled into my home for the next five days. I scrubbed the small rocks from a space between the two enormous rock outcrops that defined two sides of my camp. One side was a bowl of rocks before a steep drop-off, and the other was open to an expanse of relatively flat ground at the apex of the butte.

Once I smoothed the ground, I collected the discarded stones and built a perimeter to define my space. On the side facing the drop-off, I constructed a small altar with three rectangular stones that looked like serving dishes. I dug into my pack, pulled out an intricate Tibetan bag, and removed its contents. I placed the woven bag on my makeshift altar and set my Breitling watch on top of the bag to protect it from scratches. I placed a deck of animal spirit cards beside the bag and put a small stone on top to prevent them from blowing away.

Traditionally, animals were said to appear during vision quests, bearing messages to the Indigenous traveler. My deck, *Medicine Cards* by Sams, Carson, and Werneke, was like a bird-watcher's guide to what I might see, and it came with a booklet so I could read about the archetypal meanings. There are many ways to use this kind of oracle deck. In many cases, people draw an animal card to divine its meaning and help give insight into an aspect of their life. In my case, the cards served to help me commune with whatever spirits visited me in the desert.

I unpacked more of my gear, unhooking the camping candle lantern and placing it beside the cards. Then, practical tasks needed reviewing. I checked my water supply—all good—and then surveyed two large rocks that framed a shallow depression, spreading one of my tarps across them to create a sunshade. I spent the next while determining how to secure the tarp in place so it was stable enough to withstand a storm but easily retractable like a mechanical sunshade. I laid down the other tarp as a ground sheet and secured its sides and corners with my surplus rocks. Next, I propped one walking pole underneath the tarp like a tent pole and built a small dish of stones to secure the sharp end of the stick in the ground. The tarp was now high enough to sit underneath it, but not high enough to let the sun's light flood my shelter's sides.

I placed my leather journal and a roll of drawing pencils beneath the altar. I pulled my yellow sleeping bag from my rusty-orange backpack and stowed it in a turquoise dry sack to prevent crawling beasties from preparing a surprise I'd find when I lay down to sleep. With that, the morning evaporated in the day's heat. My temporary home was ready.

I walked to the south edge of the butte and surveyed the valley beyond. Farther on, a collection of tall, natural rock formations created a rough amphitheater. Beyond it was another range of jagged hills. To the west, a wall of steep hills. The east revealed more mountains so distant that they formed the horizon. The north led back across the valley floor to our launching point.

I stripped off my sweater and opened a bottle of water. Twenty disposable bottles of water were sequestered in their makeshift refrigerator, and two more liters were in the water pouch in my backpack.

I was excited now, ticking off tasks and looking to establish structure in the chaotic topography. Exposure to the noonday sun was a battle I would lose. I crawled into my shelter and contemplated what to do next. I reconsidered my construction effort. Incremental improvements busied my mind as I subconsciously avoided the obvious. I wasn't here to build protection from my world. I was here to expose myself to it. I was here to let the sun bake me, to let the night cold seep into my heart as my body withered from lack of nutrients. I was here to strip down, not build up.

I reasoned that travel during the day was foolhardy. I would keep major excursions and exploration to early morning or late afternoon. The rest of the time, I would spend under my canopy, meditating, writing, or drawing. I got out my sketching pencils and doodled in my journal.

Drawing and painting were something that used to light me up, but I'd stopped years before. I had a fondness for birds and had studied chickadees in university. They were resourceful little creatures with an elephant-like memory used to encode the location of cached food that would see them through the lean months of winter. These feathery golf balls could survive northern climates, skipping the typically mandatory migration south. Unlike them, I had chosen to go south. Not a migration of necessity but one of choosing.

From my birdwatching and studies, a love for painting birds had sprung: blue jays, black-capped chickadees, hawks, kingfishers, and so on. But I stopped painting after a casual friend looked at my pieces and critiqued them. "These birds look like they should be on wine labels," the casual friend had said.

Was my art a pleasant decoration that conveyed the essence of grapes? It made me feel like my art was commercial or contrived. Instead of a mirror to reflect our being, it was a plastic version of reality. I quit painting soon after.

While out here, I decided to rekindle my passion for art and disregard my critics.

Under my tarp, I leaned back against the tall rock, using my backpack as a cushion, and settled in to draw and write, facing the shadows in my south. I unwrapped the leather strip that bound my journal closed and flipped the wrinkled pages until I found a fresh one. I recorded memories of my council of allies. I reflected on my life and my marriage. I considered my career. Most of my scribblings swung between unrealized revelations and whining, first-world nonsense. It was mainly questions or snippets of thought. It was contrived, designed to portray me as the victim, but I knew that it was possible I was the antagonist from someone else's vantage point.

I put the pencil down, placed my hat over my eyes, and napped on and off through the hot afternoon.

I don't remember much about the first night, other than feeling nervous. I placed my backpack in a dry sack and my boots in another.

My sleeping bag was rated for this climate, but my ground sheet and inflatable mattress provided little insulation from the cold earth. I wrapped myself up in the Navajo blanket, then lay down in my sleeping bag and zipped it up. I kept my long underwear on and pulled my wool Sherpa hat tight. I quickly learned that the night brought more risk from cold than from the predators I'd so feared. The cold was even more draining than the lack of sustenance.

I woke early the following day. The constellation Orion was above the horizon, and Sirius, easily found by following the three stars of Orion's Belt, shimmered. Sirius was a binary star—a smaller star orbiting its more significant mate. *Two stars, one light,* I thought. Beyond these astrological artifacts, I knew Polaris—the North Star—and Ursa Major, commonly known as the Big Dipper because of its distinctive pot-and-handle configuration.

In my first year of university, I took an astronomy class and fell in love with the subject. However, I quickly realized that my mathematical skills were inadequate for a study that required advanced geometry and physics. As much as I loved the night sky, astronomy was relegated to a casual hobby.

I was cold to the bone. I put on another anorak and a sweater and tried some yoga poses to stimulate blood flow through my muscles and to generate heat. As I did, a hint of light peeked over the mountains to the east. Sirius became my bringer of light. Light meant the day had arrived. The day meant the sun would rise, and I would feel warmth again.

Like an ectothermic creature, I begged the sun to resurrect my body. I watched as the sun broke over the horizon—dark to light, cold to warm—and opened my wool blanket to receive its energy. I stood like a lizard, taking in the sun's life-giving rays.

I meditated atop a large rock nearby as the sky broke into a pale-turquoise hue. I was grateful to have made it through my first solo day and thankful I had not encountered the land's predators. I tried to push all thoughts from my mind, but the sun on my face drove an uncontrollable smile. I appreciated the celestial fiery globe in a way I never had before. It was not something to take for granted or a nuisance for sensitive eyes and skin. It was my ally. It was a life-giver and a welcome companion.

I returned to my camp and discovered unnerving depressions in the ground. All around my sleeping place were paw prints. Large ones. They appeared at the base of my headstone rock and moved about my camp. It was hard to follow them. I had been visited by something larger than a coyote. It must have been a mountain lion.

This unseen nocturnal visitor shook me. A magnificent killer had visited sometime in the night, surveyed my presence, and deemed me unworthy of eating. I was elated and somewhat insulted.

I shuffled through my animal spirit cards until I found

the mountain lion card and checked the guide for its meaning. The mountain lion symbolizes power, resilience, and the ability to overcome obstacles. It speaks of the need to tap into one's inner strength and reserves to face the challenges of the waking world. I thanked the feline for bringing this message without taking payment in the form of my flesh.

I packed my bedroll into its dry sack and manually retracted my tarp into a neat bundle over my headstone rock. Then, I gathered my day pack and set out on a hike. I traded my wool cap for my brimmed hat, gathered my leather gloves and hiking poles, and set out down the north face of the butte.

I spent part of my hike completing my stone-pile duty. I made my way there and found the capstone placed neatly in front of the pile. I picked up the stone and put it back on top. Sam was safe. I wanted him to know the same about me. We'd both made it to day two. My obligation complete, I turned to navigate around the base of my home butte, heading for the mountains I had seen south of me. I would spend my morning exploring.

Crossing the small plain and entering the rocky foothills, I explored, searching for the remains of a shamanic site rumored to be in the area. Though I found remnants of mining tools and a rusted bear trap, which proved that long-ago prospectors had worked in this area, I came up empty on finding the site. After navigating back to camp, I undertook my first ceremony. To protect myself from the lures of the world's trappings, I would release my dependence on fake measures of value. My symbol of this severance was the surrendering of my inheritance. I would sacrifice my Breitling wristwatch.

A ritual of severance breaks the energy of activities, dependencies, or relationships. Another way to think of severance is as the termination of a contract that no longer serves its signers. The object of the severance is usually symbolic. We have all likely enacted this rite of passage without considering it a ritual. The jilted lover returns personal belongings to their partner. Alternatively, they burn, tear apart, or dispose of those belongings in other ways. In other cases, people burn love letters or cast them in the ocean as a symbolic release from the energy of the relationship.

In essence, a ritual of severance is an intentional ending of a relationship with a person, a group of people (like work colleagues), or an object (cigarettes, alcohol, narcotics, food). The act can include burning, burying, smashing, or casting away literal or symbolic objects that must be severed. I chose the kinetic act of smashing as my ritual of severance.

In early 2012, I purchased the watch in New York City. I worked for a cybersecurity firm that focused on hedge funds and investment banks and had spent enough time in New York to recognize LaGuardia Airport by its smell. I could stand in a nondescript jet bridge with my eyes closed and know I was in the Big Apple. I walked Manhattan like a native New Yorker: making no eye contact, crossing streets based on vehicle traffic regardless of the lights, and resenting the tourists who perpetually blocked the way as they stared up into the concrete canyons of the city.

Working among wealthy people, clothes labels mattered, and shoes signaled your station. You had to wear a Brooks Brothers button-down to prove you were serious and a Patagonia vest to show you worked for a hedge fund, not a bank. I made a good salary, but it was not enough to justify a luxury watch or drive an exotic car, the marks of a fund manager.

After discovering that the jewelry shops of Forty-Seventh Street demanded around twenty thousand dollars for a used Breitling watch, I headed south to Canal Street and its peddlers of counterfeit bags, sunglasses, and watches. There, the buyer risked arrest, dealing in fast-food-restaurant washrooms or side alleys as the sellers hawked their faux couture. I challenged one seller after another to produce a Breitling knockoff.

They kept to the cheap Rolex lookalikes, with arms that ticked instead of sweeping around the watch face.

Breitling was a specialist's choice—it was made for mariners and pilots. It was a hyperaccurate timepiece designed for real uses. To me, it retained its true purpose and had not been hijacked by more popular brands hoarded by an elite few. My choice told the seller that I was serious and not an average tourist looking for a fake Burberry.

I finally stumbled upon a merchant who knew someone with what I was looking for.

"No Rolex. I want a Breitling." I stood firm. After a few more attempts to sell me tourist junk, he gave in.

"Wait here," he instructed. He opened a panel adorned with watches and sunglasses and went into the back of his shop. I waited patiently, wondering if he'd tired of my demand and was ignoring me until I went away. A few moments later, an elderly Asian lady emerged behind me and asked me to confirm my selection.

"You are the one who wants the fancy watch?" she asked as much as she announced.

"I want the Breitling Chronomat. Can you get me one?"

"It will cost you—not like this stuff," she said as she waved her hand at the backdrop of fake Gucci and Burberry.

We haggled the price down to $500. She clicked her teeth in faux resentment, made a call, and said, "Follow me."

We made our way through the tourists along Canal Street toward Chinatown. We turned into a crowded alley of Asian restaurants and grocery stores. I was lost. The elderly lady spun around to face me after what seemed like too long and told me to wait there. She demanded the cash, and I handed it over reluctantly—would I ever see the watch now? I missed that she was looking past me, and she nodded as I handed over the cash. A younger Asian man approached and pushed a small paper bag into my hands. I looked inside, and the watch was there. I looked up. The old lady and the young fellow were gone, vanished into the throng.

At first, I was proud of my watch. It was so authentic that it could have been legitimate. Perhaps it was. If so, the watch was likely stolen or a counterfeit made by a professional. Its legitimate construction only made it more fake. It spoke of money and success I didn't have.

The more I wore it, the more it symbolized fakeness. It was another proxy, and I came to resent it. Worse, it was a representation of a society by which I was becoming disenfranchised. It was a metafraud. One night in a restaurant with colleagues and customers, a coworker pointed me out to a client who asked, "The guy with the Breitling?" When she told me about the interaction, I felt hollow, knowing I had betrayed myself. I stopped wearing the watch.

I began my first ritual by calling back and cleansing my energy.

"I release all energy that does not come from love back to its source, cleansed and without attachment," I intoned, like a mantra. "And I call back my energy from all sources, cleansed and without attachment."

I repeated my mantra to clear my mind. Then, as Sparrow Hart had shown me, I smudged using a small bundle of sage sitting in an abalone shell and a crow feather. I wafted the smoke around my legs, under my groin, around my torso and arms, then finally around my head. I was cleansing my chakras from the first, or root, chakra at my tailbone to the highest chakra, my crown chakra, at the top of my head.*

---

* According to Indian tantric yoga, there are seven main energy centers, or chakras, that run from the base of the torso to the top of the skull. Each chakra has a theme or purpose. The root chakra is located at the base of the spine and is associated with safety, grounding, basic needs, and belonging and is represented by the color red. The second chakra (orange), the sacral chakra, is located just below the navel and is associated with creativity and sensation. The solar plexus chakra (yellow) is located in the upper abdomen, as its name suggests, and is linked to personal power,

I was ready. I was exhilarated. I placed the watch on a flat stone. This first ritual marked the formal beginning of my vision quest, in which I made a one-way commitment to my journey. Once the watch was destroyed, there was no repairing my valuable item. There was no turning back.

I read the section of my letter of intent that spoke of severances and believing in myself. Calling in my energy and taking back my authenticity, I meditated on the need to see myself as others do and to be sincere, regardless of whether it alienated me or cost me my career.

"Watch, you represent greed and insincerity. I purchased you as a symbol of success that would speed me to acceptance within a group of people from whom I no longer seek approval or admiration." I spoke with confidence. The energy of what was to come was buzzing and pooling in readiness. It floated around me like sage smoke.

"Wealth and its trappings do not represent me," I said. "I will not rely on a measure of wealth to determine my value. My severance is to see myself as who I am. To see myself as others do: a talented and kind man." I paused as if to let the message absorb the intent of my words. "I will no longer wilt with frequent praise."

I folded the letter and tucked it back into my notebook, which I then placed on the altar—my anvil.

I picked up a baseball-size rock to use as a hammer. I rolled the rock in my hand, feeling its cracks. The dust coated my hands, serving to increase my grip like a weightlifter or gymnast does with chalk.

---

self-esteem, and confidence. The heart chakra (green) is fourth, located in the center of the chest and tied to love, compassion, and forgiveness. Communication, self-expression, and truth are associated with the fifth chakra, the throat chakra (blue). Positioned on the forehead between the eyebrows is the third eye, or sixth chakra, which is considered to be the center of intuition and insight and is represented by indigo. The seventh chakra, the crown chakra (violet), is located on the top of the head and connects us to higher consciousness and spiritual awareness.

"I will not drape myself in material items that signal monetary success. I will be me, and not the expectation of people for whom I have no respect. I will gain my acceptance through love and kindness."

With that, I smashed the rock down on my watch, sending it bouncing into the air and back down on the rock altar. The face was scratched, but it was mostly intact.

I struck again. And again. My insides were tingling! I was smashing down the wall of self-imposed dependency. It was my perestroika.

First, the glass face broke free and splintered. Then the dial around the face split from its housing and rolled off the altar. The watch and all it represented were surrendering. I pounded the rock down several more times and watched as the arms snapped from their anchor. With repeated strikes, the inner gears fell from the housing like intestines dripping from a stricken animal. With each assault, pieces of metal and springs flew through the air like a mechanical mist. My exhilaration flamed at the destruction and liberation as my mind stood like a spectator questioning my sanity. I smashed an expensive item for a reason that most people would find ridiculous. There I was, eviscerating my possessions to break the shackles holding back my expansion.

Once the watch was unrecognizable, I gathered the pieces and placed them on my altar. I had taken the first energetic step toward Source. My ember glowed. I sacrificed a valuable possession and a symbol of my drift from what mattered. I took my first step back to my true self.

Before I left, I planned to dispose of what once was my watch. It was natural metal, and I would throw the refuse off the cliff when I was ready to leave. For now, the broken shards were a reminder of my commitment and courage. Its destruction marked the beginning of my transformation. Broken, it had a new purpose without any unhealthy attachment to my psyche.

As night fell, I began my evening ritual. I rolled back my sun-blocking tarp, making a bundle that I secured to the top of the rock with a parachute cord. I was now exposed to the sky. The sun was in the west, and the tarp no longer provided shade. Soon, the mountains would swallow the sun and usher in the stars.

I pulled my sleeping bag and Navajo blanket from the dry sack, replacing them with my backpack and boots, and laid them out on my ground sheet. I lit the small candle lantern sitting on my altar. It threw only a small amount of light. It could illuminate a small tent, but much of its light was lost without a surface on which to reflect.

I made an entry in my notebook about day one. *I am on the right path,* I wrote. I had taken two significant steps. The first was my walk into the valley alone. The second was my severance of dependency. Once finished, I crawled into my sleeping bag and extinguished my lantern.

As I lay down, I pulled my wool hat tight and then felt around on the ground to find my headlamp. I placed it on my hat for safekeeping, just in case I needed to illuminate a nocturnal visitor.

I rolled over to take in the sunset. I was adapting to the circadian rhythm of the earth. I rose with the sun and slept with its setting. I was losing touch with the sense of time that had bound me to a nine-to-five lifestyle. My inner ember glowed to keep me company.

CHAPTER FIVE

Snakes, Shadows, and Surrender

Death Valley, California, Days 6–8

The following morning, I woke to look for Sirius and shivered, waiting for the sun. I performed my morning meditation, prepared my camp for the day, and set out to connect with Sam via the silent confirmation of life through our stone pile.

Standing in the dry riverbed, I contemplated which direction to explore. Today, I decided to travel up the river and into the mountains to the west. I was confident of my solitude.

After returning to Baker Creek following our solo time, I learned that the western mountains—where Sam had initially camped—had been unsuitable because of rain runoff, and Sam had relocated to the amphitheater instead. There, he'd found broken bowls, hieroglyphs, and arrowheads—that was the home of shamanic relics. He left them where he saw them, just like our covenant demanded. At first, I was envious. He had found the remnants of the shamans I had searched for. In hindsight, I realized I wasn't ready to experience them. He had made this journey multiple times—perhaps he was.

I began the arduous trek up the mountain, following the riverbed. As the grade became steeper, I scrambled over jams of car-size rocks. The riverbed turned to slow steps of sand risers and treads. At the top, there was a landing of flat rocks. My first step tipped a plate-size stone, and I stumbled. I heard an ominous rattle and stopped to survey my foot placement. Quick movement flashed in the shadows of two low-lying rocks in front of my foot.

It was the ideal place for a serpent to find shelter for the night. Alternatively, it was a good place to lie in wait for prey to stumble by. The snake rattled again. I slowly lifted my foot off the unstable stone, like I was trying to escape the fate of a triggered landmine. I moved slowly and stepped back from the snake's lair. After a few more steps, never breaking eye contact with its hiding place, the snake and I parted ways.

I took a wide circle as I contemplated my luck. It is dangerous to disrupt the doormat of a deadly serpent. Luckily, the coiled beast thought better of wasting precious venom on me. Twice, I had been deemed unworthy of the attention of local predators. Perhaps the snake was not there to attack me. I meant it no harm, so in turn, it left me alone. We could pass with mutual respect, without resorting to aggression to prove our superiority. I continued my climb until I faced a rock wall smoothed long ago by running water. It had flowed over the cliff above me to form the torrent that had carved the riverbed below. Given I had no climbing gear or ropes, this was the termination point. I turned east and headed back down the mountain, giving my slithering companion a wide berth.

The sun was well on its way to the western mountains.

Its heat was still formidable as I left the shade of the nearby rocks and staggered back to my camp. The climb up to my home butte was laborious. I was glad for the shade of my tarp. I drank water, rested, and took off my dust-covered boots.

I removed my animal spirit deck again and learned that the rattlesnake's message is transformation, healing, and re-birth. Others believe the rattlesnake is a warning to take heed of our surroundings. The appearance of a rattlesnake that doesn't cause harm suggests we accept change, not fear it, and consider what drives this change. The unaggressive rattlesnake asks us to reflect on how we have been treated and how we have treated others.

I reflected on my mistrust of people. I often assumed peo-ple would betray or leave me. I could be sharp. More often than I was proud of, I would preemptively strike with a clinical anger designed to deliver my own form of fast-acting venom. Close family members had felt the bite. Those who understood me knew it was my fear speaking. It turned out, I had more in common with the rattlesnake than I wanted to admit. I lacked its rattle and stripes, but I came with my own set of risks for anyone who got too close. A trickle of sweat ran down my head in a futile attempt to irrigate my surroundings before evaporating.

I felt the sting of my spiteful words as I reflected on loved ones I had verbally struck. I thought of a high school friend, Danny, whom I had treated poorly before leaving for univer-sity. I was young and arrogant and had been cruel over some-thing pointless. I'd struck neither in defense nor in purposeful aggression. The rattlesnake was wiser than I was. I wasted my precious venom for no purpose.

Danny had been a close friend. Moreover, he was always the one who stayed behind with me whenever I was caring for my brother. After my parents divorced, I was often Craig's primary caregiver. Because of his disorders, he could not walk without assistance, needed to be fed, and required almost around-the-clock care usually reserved for toddlers much younger than he. Danny loved Craig, and he loved me enough never to leave me alone when I was stuck looking after my brother.

Before I left Toronto to attend university in London, Ontario, Danny and I had a trip planned to his friend's cottage in Muskoka. It would be a boys' weekend. At the last minute, my friend Jasper, from another social circle, asked if he could come. Hours before we were to leave, I checked with Danny.

"Man, can Jasper come with us?" I asked Danny.

It was instantly clear that he did not want Jasper tagging along. "I'm not sure," he responded. "The cottage is small, and I don't feel right inviting extra people without permission."

"What's the big deal?" I said, ignoring Danny's hesitation. "He can sleep on the floor."

"They need notice to prepare," he sheepishly responded. I felt caught between two friend groups, and my patience was low. I just wanted to get going and did not want the hassle this was turning into.

"To prepare what, exactly?" I asked curtly.

Danny was caught off guard. He did not want Jasper to come, and I knew it. He was flailing for an excuse to keep him out of our weekend plans. Danny was a smart guy, but he was not quick on his toes when it came to arguments.

Jasper was from money and could be a snob. He was hyperintelligent and occasionally lacked tact. People had to fit his view of the world, not the other way around, and he could be uncompromising to the point of condescension. Danny and his gang were down-to-earth types who lived blue-collar lives. I was a bit in the middle, able to adapt to either social bracket. I did not come from a wealthy background, but I had the smarts to make my way into a well-to-do postsecondary educational institution.

I knew this was oil and water. I was forcing this brackish mix.

"Prepare what?" I repeated. "I'm not asking them to build an addition or give up their master bedroom for him." At eighteen, self-righteousness is as unyielding as it is fluid, easily contorting to fit any given situation. Somehow, everything seems black and white at that age.

"I don't know, like bring extra bedding or buy more groceries." Danny fumbled, looking for footing as my flurry of words kept pushing him off balance.

We continued, my jabs met with half-hearted parries. I kept pushing Danny to give in. But he would not. He seemed disappointed I had asked. He could have been envious of my friend, or perhaps nervous about his attitude, and did not want Jasper there.

The problem was me, and I knew it. I had grown increasingly arrogant as university approached. I was forgetting the support and compassion Danny showed me growing up, just to impress another friend. It was a sad display of disloyalty. Danny deserved better. He deserved the type of loyalty he had always shown me.

"Got it. You do not like him because he is rich," I snapped.

Danny cried, "That's not true—"

But I cut him off. "Yeah, you're just worried your other buddies might be washing his car one day, right?"

Danny's eyes were welling up. I was a puffed-up asshole, looking down my nose at the one person who had always held me on a pedestal. I had no right.

"Fine. Have a nice trip. See you when you get back," I snapped. "Or not."

With that, I turned and walked out of Danny's life.

There I sat in the desert, thousands of miles away from where he lived, last I knew, rehashing a moment I had spent years agonizing over. Danny had always stayed with me, and I had abandoned him. And then I left for university, without ever resolving the fissure I had created between us.

I drew a deep breath and let it out. "I miss you, my friend," I said to Danny, hoping he would hear my remorse and forgive me.

As I had done the day before, I started my next ritual, calling back my energy and smudging to clear the air. I inhaled the sage vapors. Today, I would perform another ritual of severance, but this time, I was going to conduct a burial.

Like a funeral, this was a service to return the living to the earth, reabsorbing the energy of the loss and giving back to Mother Earth as an offering to encourage rebirth. I tore a page from my notebook and wrote FEAR on it. I placed this offering on the altar and flipped through the remaining pages of my notebook to find a passage Sparrow Hart had taught us days earlier in Big Cedar.

"Circles of air, circles of stone," I started. I picked up a piece of rose quartz from my stone circle. "Earth circles, and night follows day."

I placed the rose quartz on the snippet of paper. With two hands, I wrapped the paper around the stone and clasped the completed offering between my hands as I brought them to my heart in prayer.

"We bury our seeds, we bury our bones," I said, cupping my offering in my hands and scraping a shallow grave in the sand underneath my altar. I let the offering of paper and stone fall gently into the hole.

I breathed in and out and then brushed sand over the grave to complete the burial. I paused to bring my hands back to my heart in prayer and looked up to the sky. "While sacred birds circle and pray," I whispered.

"With this severance, I bury fear. I let go of past hurts and betrayals. I will embrace opportunities, believe the best in people, and avoid striking out in the fear of abandonment or hurt. I will take the medicine of Rattlesnake into my heart."

"Thank you, my friend," I said to Danny again. "Please hear my words and forgive me."

—

The fourth day alone in the desert dawned, bringing relief from the cold. I had fallen into a rhythm of greeting the sun, meditating, and tending to the stone pile, but the fatigue of chilled sleep and a water-based diet was taking its toll. My initial zest for exploration was waning. My senses were dulled, but not enough to keep the boredom at bay.

I was perpetually hungry and tired. I forced away thoughts of food. The last thing I wanted to do was fuel my hunger pangs. I would sing a song or sip water, waiting for my stomach rumbles to slip into the background of my awareness.

I had been on my own for days, and my connection to the world was slipping. For all I knew, the world beyond this valley was a figment of my imagination. My thoughts drifted in and out of focus, like an untuned radio station.

Midday was spent under my tarp, avoiding the heat of the sun. The sun and I had a love-hate relationship. The stars, on the other hand, kept me company during the night. My binary star, Sirius, was not as duplicitous as the sun. Sirius assured me I had made it through the cold night. The sun was then there to warm me before having a go at baking me to death.

I spent time sketching rocks and plants. My thoughts drifted to my marriage and relationship. I was unhappy and unsatisfied, and I was also half committed. I always had a plan B waiting in the wings. Nevertheless, I stayed because I did not want to sacrifice my daughter's happiness for my own. I drove to work each day, convincing myself to remain in a paper-thin marriage until my kid went off to university. Becoming an empty nester would allow me to fly the coop.

But that wasn't any way to live. I needed to settle my life and get things in order. I needed to face my responsibilities and consider the future I wanted. Inspired by my brief morning walk, I began writing in my journal and composed the following poem:

> *Our lives flow on a river at once, defining yet*
> *guided by the walls of this steep canyon.*
> *At times, we rush toward each other like the*
> *torrents in the rapids.*
> *At others, we drift away, passengers on the*
> *gently meandering swell.*
> *And like this, we have traveled for as long as*
> *it took the water to carve this canyon that*
> *now marks its path.*
> *And through all, we never forget our intent.*
> *The river forks around rocky outcrops.*
> *And when the wind-swept towers separate us,*
> *look to our stars that dance around one*
> *another, reminding us never to lose sight.*
> *Our times together bring the warmth of a*
> *desert spring, and apart, the sun's fall*
> *brings a lonely chill.*
> *Yet through the night, the coyotes call to one*
> *another, a reminder that in darkness,*
> *together, we still carry our light.*
> *The two forks of this river come together when*
> *they are meant to and never before.*
> *They must each carve out their path to form a*
> *deep Sapphire Lake where they eternally*
> *unite.*

The poem was about love, but not simply the romantic kind. It was about two star-crossed lovers who could not be together in the *now*, waiting until the time was right. Some would orbit each other for eternity. Some would make it across their soulful Lagrangian point and combine into a light brighter than their sum. Two stars, one light.

Below the surface, it was a metaphor for the west and north shields. It was two rivers, the purpose of the individual and the sweet medicine given to the community. It was about a ripening of fruit along the medicine wheel. Both parties had to come to their fruition—the giver and the receiver spinning a flywheel in equilibrium.

The Sapphire Lake was a place in my mind. It was the calm waters of a tranquil evening. It was the moon reflected on the infinite depth of the water as the crackle of a warm fire sings to the embers ascending to mingle with the stars above. It was peace. Safety. It was a place where my inner ember whispered to me, and I heard its message.

I returned my leather journal to my improvised altar and promptly fell asleep.

When I awoke, the sun was setting over the mountaintops, which glowed with the last of the day's light. I wandered around my camp to collect the readily available scrub and whatever meager wood I could find to build a fire. Tonight, I would need it. I was calling in the darkness.

About an hour after sunset, the air rumbled with drums of distant thunder. To the west, the sky lit with blurred flashes of lightning. I was grateful for the mountains between me and the tempest, as they held the impending thunderstorm at bay. The flashes of lightning asserted the storm's intention of turning my dusty solitude into a soup of sand and rocks seasoned with my hovering fears.

In a show of epic power, the storm raged mere miles from my camp, yet only a few drops of rain ever fell near me. The lightning sparked and pulsed, illuminating the clouds. To me, it seemed there was an invisible wall of atmospheric contempt containing the storm. Nevertheless, the storm's presence was a reminder that something ominous was lurking.

Calling in the darkness was a ceremony to invite my fears and demons to sit with me. I was the host, yet it would be their agenda. Darkness was not fueled by thoughts of slithering snakes, crawling spiders, or made-up demons and monsters. Instead, it focused on real inner fears. The ritual was meant to integrate what I had exiled and denied.

While our daily lives enforce conformity, we often overlook our limbic selves, which exist beyond the labels of "normal" or "deviant" or "good" or "evil." Our limbic system is what keeps us alive. This ancient part of our brain drives survival, regardless of whether our conscious thoughts, personal biases, or societal norms contradict its methods. Like an atom with its positrons and electrons, we are bound to our neurological-existence engine, which at times can conflict with our social obligations. Sometimes, this shadow side of humanity manifests in arguments over a parking space or impatient remarks while standing in line at the bank. At other times in human history, our collective shadow has draped the world in war.

To summon the darkness meant facing these base urges and fears. It was also an invitation to address unsatiated desires, psychological wounds, or emotions I'd been keeping in check. As the name suggests, this ritual should be performed in the dark, at best shortly after dusk, when light surrenders its domain over the earth.

I waited patiently, suspended in a bowl of blackness, defined only by a dim cobalt glow that marked the jagged horizon. Each flash of lightning illuminated the mountains around me like dragon's teeth, confirming my place as its next meal. Each sporadic drop of rain was its saliva, basting me for the inevitable.

I set alight a small pile of sagebrush to keep me company and, taking deep breaths, performed a prayer to call back my energy, as I had done before performing the other rituals.

As a kid, I was always scared of the dark. An unlit basement was an abyss from which the tendril of dread would reach out and pull me into its inky abode. Now, I sat in the middle of Death Valley, where I should be concerned about the dark and the real creatures that lurked under its cover. It felt different.

"Am I prepared for this?" I asked myself.

My meager fire offered a bubble of light but did little to expel the surrounding void of pitch-black desert. Within the bubble was warmth and a contrast-rich stage upon which the shadows danced, music of the flames. Loose rocks and the nearby outcrop appeared to slither from the light, as if moving to their preferred darkness. Behind me was the void: nothingness defined by a sliver of horizon that transitioned to a living night sky.

In the desert, the night sky is not washed out by city lights. It glows to its full potential. It is a tapestry of countless stars, each one with its unique hue and intensity. Nevertheless, no matter how brilliant, the stars taunted me from a distance too great to provide warmth, too far to show me what waited patiently just out of sight. The darkness was patient. Moreover, it knew nothing would interfere with our rendezvous.

Despite my hours of toil collecting dead scrub, the bubble of warmth and self-assurance offered by my fire collapsed, darkness seeping back in to claim its reign over my time alone. I again found myself waiting in the dark for my guests to arrive.

Shivering, I pulled my hat down over my ears, zipped up my jacket, and pulled my scarf over my mouth. Even with my layers of modern gear, I was freezing, my breath dissipating into the night.

I looked up at the tapestry of stars. The haze of the Milky Way was visible, like a diagonal scar across the sky. In the cold air, the stars shimmered. The sky had looked much this same way thousands of years ago, when Indigenous peoples walked this valley. The signs were there nearby in the valley, undisturbed for decades and beyond my discovery.

The stars were ancient and had witnessed countless lives unfold. They had seen cultures and empires rise and fall. They were witnesses to the evolution of countless species and their predictable decline into extinction. Their role was to remind us that time fills a scale not comprehensible to a single entity, whether a grain of sand, a plant cell, or a human being. Their distance became a chilling reminder of my inconsequentiality. What would the stars witness tonight, in the eyeblink of my existence? I cleared my throat, then paused to look around one last time at my cold surroundings.

"I am ready," I announced to Darkness. "Come show yourself."

My words swirled between the rocks of my outcrop and faded into blackness around me. Each syllable had the longevity of my short-lived fire. Darkness swallowed my words as soon as they left my mouth. It was like yelling in an anechoic chamber. I was supposed to wait until I sensed something.

"Some people will see shadows near them, say, beside a tree, and have the feeling that something is there," Sparrow Hart had explained as part of our preparations. "Others might hear words in their mind, forming a conversation that illuminates an inner knowledge of their fears."

Facing the darkness is not simply a one-way exchange. It is a negotiation between a primal fear and your desire to live free of such shackling dread. I imagined two players on a stage: one, the energy of the darkness, and the other, its person.

"I am your rejection," Darkness says, embodying the energy of rejection. "No one chooses you. I want you to live without acceptance from those you love the most."

"I will not accept that," the person retorts. "The price is too high."

"Then I want you always to forgo meaningful relations so you remain alone," Darkness demands.

Again, the person denies this demand. "Your price is too high."

After several similar exchanges, Darkness makes its final offer: "I want you to acknowledge that power I have held in your life. You're a perpetual pleaser, constantly seeking approval from people. Even the ones who never deserved your loyalty."

The recognition slaps the person. The truth is visceral. After a pause, the person speaks: "I can accept your bargain. I acknowledge you, Darkness called rejection, and honor the power you have over me."

To seal the bargain, the person offers to remember the power of rejection on the winter solstice and light a sage bundle as tribute. In that moment of recognition, the person takes back power from Darkness.

Summoning the darkness is realizing you can turn on the light in your basement while still recognizing the times you feared descending the stairs and how fear controlled your childhood.

I repeated my invitation, and again the words were immediately absorbed by the night. Nothing came. Or so I thought. Then I heard a movement to my right. By the outcrop, a shadow seemed to retreat into the backside of the rock wall. It was low to the ground, about the size of a dog. Was that panting I heard?

I stared at the rocks, trying to discern one shape among the myriad of shadows. *A coyote?* I wondered. Was I experiencing what Sparrow Hart had described back at base camp? Was my visitor taking visual form?

If it were a coyote, I should be concerned. For some reason, I was not.

"Bandit?" I called out, suddenly thinking of my dog who'd

died a few years earlier. She was a mixed breed that looked remarkably like a coyote, with a curly husky tail held high. Her name referred to the dark band of fur across her eyes. She resembled a cartoon thief, though without the striped-prison garb and bag of cash.

"Is that you, girl?" I asked, catching a glimpse of movement on top of the rock wall. "I miss you, girl."

Nothing. I felt a pang for my dog. She was my first pet, and I missed having her at my side. I shifted and stood up. What had I seen among the rocks? Was it a nocturnal predator or the spirit of my deceased family pet? Either way, I felt eerily calm and safe given my contradictory surroundings. I felt somehow protected.

I shivered again while surveying my camp. The familiar rocks gave way to the horizon, with a dazzling starscape above. This wasn't how I expected the summoning to play out. I expected fear, screaming, and an emotional reckoning.

It seemed nothing was taking up my invitation. The mountain lion had thought better of me. The rattlesnake had not been bothered to strike. Now, my own darkness refused my invitation.

I dusted off my pants, then walked over to the dry sacks that stored my sleeping gear. I shook out my sleeping bag and placed it on my ground tarp. I removed my boots and knocked them together to loosen the dust and sand before placing them in the sack to prevent snakes from taking up residence.

"It was good to see you, girl," I said, deciding to believe it had been Bandit, as I slid into my sleeping bag and shivered. I pulled down my hat and rolled onto my side to sleep, reminded that visions do not arrive on a Hollywood red carpet when you ask for them. They come only when the traveler is ready to receive the message.

I felt a flicker of doubt. Was all this just bullshit? Perhaps my critics were right, and I was wasting my time alone in the desert. I wondered if I should not have lit the fire before starting the ceremony. Had my fire served as a warning sign for Darkness to stay away? Perhaps I wasn't ready to receive or confront my shadow self. Was I being too superstitious about a ritual designed to commune with the supernatural? Yes. It was about facing one's darkness, not literal ghosts or demons—right?

In the morning, I put away my sleeping gear and grabbed my walking pole. I had to return the capstone to our stone pile in the dry riverbed to ensure my invisible partner knew that I was safe, at least for today. Trekking there, I relived the moment in the dark, remembering how an overwhelming feeling of safety had accompanied the shadow. Something had happened. It was not what I had expected. In that moment, I wished Bandit *were* with me.

Once my morning duty was complete, I dusted off my gloved hands and began hiking up the riverbed, climbing over boulders and walking toward the mountains to my north. As I climbed, a logjam of rocks and boulders blocked my way. To circumvent the obstacle, I climbed the side of the river embankment carved by the rushing waters of a recent storm. As I planted my walking pole on a stable rock, my footing slipped, and I fell ten feet down the slope.

Suddenly, I was lying prostrate on what felt like an undulating waterbed mattress of sand along the washout. My head bobbed on this nonexistent current, and my vision was blurry. Wiping my mouth and spitting out sand seemed the only thing I could do. I slowly turned my head to survey my walking pole, still tethered to my wrist. It was twisted at an unnatural angle.

I lay my head back down and stared at the sky. The sun to the left was higher in the sky than I remembered when I'd made the stone pile. Before I'd fallen, the sun had still been blocked by my home butte, the dark mound that commanded my little region of the valley. Now it was blazing above the mount. *I passed out.* How much time had I lost?

Any movement of my head jarred loose, stabbing pains, so I moved slowly. I shifted my legs, and my left knee flared in agony. Bending my leg was worse than moving my head. I could bend it, but it was tight and sore. Thankfully, there was no blood on my hiking pants. I dodged that bullet. Since I could move it, I assumed it was not broken.

Still, a dull fear was bubbling up. My walking pole was broken, I had injured my leg, and I had no idea where I was. It took some time and considerable effort to sit upright, but I made it halfway to my ambitious goal of standing. I shifted my legs, and they moved as commanded. My one leg barked resistance to any order, but even its grievances could not convince me that I was seriously injured.

I spent the next while (who knew how long) getting to my feet. I balanced on my right leg and slowly bent over to pick up my walking pole. It hadn't been as lucky as my knee. The pole was dislocated and snapped at its midpoint. One of the elastic joint connectors had snapped, and the metal tube of the mid-section was flattened and bent. My multitool knife was insufficient for this kind of repair. The pole had seen its last trek. It was now junk that needed to be carried out of the desert when I left. I still had the other walking pole from the pair back at my encampment. I just needed to get back.

The desert had issued its warning, much like the speed-limit sign on an interstate onramp. *Take it easy and be mindful of injury. Otherwise, you will be dinner for one of your many predators.* Regardless, I was too physically weak to risk continuing my hike. My knee was done with long treks. At least for now. I needed what constitution I had left to haul myself back to camp.

I surveyed my surroundings. My butte stood like a fortress wall. Even in a confused state, I knew my temporary camp was at the top. I headed toward its base, limping the mile or so and then climbing the dark rocks that stood stark against the monotone taupe of the valley. As I climbed, something felt wrong.

"This has to be the right hill," I spoke aloud.

It was the only dark stone butte in the area, but the slope felt unfamiliar to me. The rocky outcrops, paths lined with loose rose quartz, and stepping stones were not quite the same. My knee hurt, and my badly needed walking pole was out of commission, but worse, I was disoriented. I was out of phase with my body and my physical surroundings.

Again, I was reminded that the desert was a trickster.

Distance is a mirage of undulating destinations, like waves on a beach. At one moment, a desired landmark looks close by. Yet the desert ground is as unlevel as it is unstable. Each step brings the risk of sinking into the den of some subterranean critter, and washouts cut scars through the landscape. Each presents a canyon to descend and ascend. What looked like an hour's hike as the crow flies could take the better part of a day, depending on the obstacles you encountered.

Time in the desert is muted into a gentle melody of sunrise, high noon, evening, and sunset. The only consistency is the passing of the day. It was the antithesis to my regular life, which felt more like a chaotic jazz session of competing musicians hammering out a staccato of meetings, phone calls, and chores.

Through a haze of pain and exhaustion, I fought to collect and analyze what I felt were my survival facts. I could not be far from my base camp, yet nothing around me was recognizable. It must be close. I panicked. *How can I be lost?*

The sun was over the hills to the east. That meant it was still morning. I reasoned this because the air was cool enough to wear a light sweater, and my filthy wool hat was still atop my head. I did not remember conducting other daily routines, like hiding under my tarp and passing the time to avoid the midday heat. *It must still be morning,* I pleaded as much as I reasoned, petrified that I could have lost an entire day. Was my food-deprived mind that easily confused?

I sat back down on a large boulder and contemplated my options. First, I could walk, and I knew that moving was the remedy for my rapidly stiffening knee. If I could return to my camp, I would be okay. If I couldn't, I would be without water and shelter. Without the basics, it was a matter of time before a four-footed, toothy beast discovered an easy meal. I had to find my little hole among the rocks at the top of the butte.

I looked around and remembered a passage from some long-ago survival training. I needed to walk in spirals until I came upon my camp. It had to be near, somewhere, camouflaged on this now-alien hillside. I reminded myself fuzzily that my camp was at the top of a hill, not the bottom, so I needed to move upward to find my salvation. Slowly, my brain constructed a collage of memories, linked together with lines of red wool, like some detective's investigation board.

I stood and hobbled in slow circles, gradually widening out as I stumbled upward. I had moved twenty feet at most when I reached the top of the butte. Nothing was recognizable. Just a rocky hilltop with no ceremonial medicine wheel, no altar with my candle lantern, no tarp, and no dry bag containing my backpack. *What the fuck have I done?* I thought as I contemplated ending my quest and walking out of the desert for help. Assuming, of course, I knew which direction would lead me to safety.

Which direction would I even walk to escape this self-inflicted fate? East? South? I searched through my pockets for my compass, but I'd left it in my backpack. I had been hiking using essential landmarks, and it was easy to navigate when I had the mental capacity. Now, everything was different, like I had been teleported from one location in Death Valley to another. I had no references, no bearings. And only one bottle of water. That would not last me very long as the sun climbed and pounded the ground with its unrelenting heat.

Fuck it. I would rest for a while and try again later. I would replicate my spiral search pattern to find my home. For now, I was done—Death Valley, one; me, zero. I found a rock outcrop nearby and collapsed underneath it, hoping its shade would protect me from the oncoming sear of the midday sun. I would have to move to counter the sunlight shift, but at least it would work for a few hours.

Tears flowed down my cheeks, carving a canyon through the layered dirt on my face. It was like the runoff canyons and dry riverbeds carved through the arid landscape. The water was short-lived but life-giving in this barren place. I smiled, my consciousness fading as I realized the tear trails on my face were the first signs that I was becoming the desert. I was exhausted, mentally desiccated, and ready to become one with my surroundings permanently. I was surrendering.

As I drifted off to sleep, my hand dropped to my side and landed on a small pointy rock beside me. I tossed it in frustration. The rock struck something nearby and rolled back to me. The collision had made a muted sound like that of thick fabric moving. I turned my head and strained against the sun to see the dry sack containing my backpack.

I felt a jolt of energy course through my body, sharpening my mind and energizing my limbs. I looked around. I had crawled right into my base camp! My makeshift altar was nestled against some rocks, and I could see the small cave made of leaning rocks that housed my water bottle supply.

I was back! Suddenly, the foreign landscape slipped into focus, and my exhausted brain knew I was safe. I had surrendered to the process, and it saw me through. I labored to pull the Navajo blanket from the dry sack and wrapped it around me. I lay down in the sand that was my bed.

Later, I came to understand that through that travail, I had finally found the place that transcended the physical plane and led to the spiritual one. My intellect had failed me. My rational, fact-fed mind had almost misled me. Something else had guided me. What I did not know was the price for this salvation. Like the coins paid to cross the River Styx, I was about to experience the cost of crossing into the spiritual plane.

CHAPTER SIX

Visitations in the Darkness

Death Valley, California, Day 8

Despite the growing warmth of the day, I was cold, shivering in a stew of fever sweat thickened by sand. My movements were restricted to tiny shivers and convulsions. I was in that liminal place between sleep and waking. I was incapable of running from the impending tsunami of visions and reminders of the scars that mottled the clay of my being. The waters crashed onto my shore and swept me away in their powerful, cutting washouts, slicing through the thick skin I had grown to avoid facing my fears.

I had summoned the darkness. It chose to arrive on its schedule rather than mine. The concern about a campfire and performing the ritual at night the previous day showed my ignorance. Darkness and light are not limited to a physical dichotomy, like day and night.

I was prostrate. Exhausted and wasted. I was broken. As the sun's heat baked down on me, I slipped into the void.

The first of several visitors arrived.

I felt her presence and weight as she lay down beside me. Her panting came at a calming cadence. Bandit had returned from Source to help me cross the boundaries into the spiritual. She lay against me and placed her head on my hand. She sighed and relaxed into me. She knew this would be a long day, and her job was to stay with me and see me through.

"Hi, girl," I gasped through my dried-out mouth, feeling the silky cool of her dark coat. She sighed and licked her lips.

Before I'd adopted her, Bandit had been severely abused. The shelter workers explained that she had recovered from broken ribs and bruised lungs, likely the result of repeated kicking. They refused to expose more than that. But she never liked the men who visited our house, and she was primarily reactive to men wearing hats.

She was a good friend and companion. We would take long walks in the woods behind the house and then curl up in front of the fireplace to nap. She often slept at my feet, with one leg tucked and her head lying on her other outstretched paw.

Through the haze of the darkness I had called in, I recognized that I was not alone, even in the middle of this inhospitable and convicted place of death. My dog would be my guardian. I knew she would keep away the mountain lions and coyotes from the helpless wreck of her father. She would be my guide, she told me without words. Just as I had done for her years ago, she would be here to usher in my passing from this physical plane into the spiritual one. She was the pallbearer of my past, partnered with the eulogist of Darkness.

As her gentle hazel eyes closed, I wondered if a guide had

greeted my father to help him transition. Perhaps that was who had stood in the corner of the palliative care room. Who had come to aid his transition? Had my father been frightened by his guide? Had the guide been welcome, or had it been someone from his past he'd dreaded to face? And who would come to greet me now?

MY BROTHER

My brother was the first to accept my call for darkness. I was indeed experiencing corporeal manifestations. His presence was real, not some imagined feeling.

At the time, Craig was living in a Toronto condo with caregivers who looked after him around the clock. When I tried to reconcile his appearance, I could not focus. It was a contemplative version of a dream in which you tried to run but couldn't make any progress, as if wading through invisible water. I was lucid yet paralyzed when I tried to act.

There he was with me in the desert. No wheelchair. No crutches. Just sitting with me in the sand. The palsy in his arms had eased somewhat. Had he traveled? Or was I witnessing an energy that had taken his form?

Craig was almost four years younger than I was. He was born with a unique mix of disorders, mental deficiencies, and physical differences, including a combination of cerebral palsy and autism. Shortly after his birth, my father and the attending physician sat me down to explain his condition.

"Craig will never be normal," my father said, holding my hand. I cried, somehow knowing I'd been robbed of something, and my brother had too.

My father's words echoed in my mind as I returned from that childhood memory to my desert incubator. Something else was there. Like a shadow in the corner of my eye, a shimmery wisp of a presence, something was nearby. And I could feel it feeding off my suffering.

Was this Darkness a transcendent form? My brother was alive, but he was also here with me in Death Valley. Could my loss and pain coalesce like an energic dirt devil fueled by my suffering? As I struggled to find an answer, I drifted back to my childhood in the hospital.

The doctor confirmed that Craig would never be a typical brother and would require extensive medical treatment. Then, a message passed between them. The doctor nodded his urging, and my father cleared his throat.

"Craig probably will not live very long," he said, his words stabbing me with each syllable. Most of this was beyond the comprehension of a four-year-old. All I heard was that my freshly minted brother would probably die before we could play together or do what brothers were supposed to do.

I have vague recollections of that moment, a blurred swirl of memories and stories. I was angry—no, I was more than angry.

"No! It's not fair!" I raged at my father and the doctor, accusing them of lying because the truth was unthinkable. I was furious. They were talking about my brother. I took my first step in the natural role of the older brother. No one messes with my brother unless it is me.

While the doctors were wrong about Craig's life expectancy, they weren't lying about his challenges. His body lacked the gag reflex, and he would regularly choke when eating. Every meal was a crapshoot: He would choke, and my mother would bang on his chest as he went blue. After what felt like an eternity, he would cough and inhale life-giving breath. Only then would I exhale.

Every night, my parents would fold a set of clothing at the foot of my bed in case we had to rush to the hospital. Some nights I woke disoriented by my parents shaking me, commanding that I dress because Craig had stopped breathing again or had a seizure. We would pack him in the car and rush to the hospital. My father would speed along Leslie Street in Toronto, the hazard lights blinking, like we were a deputized police car. Once there, we'd rush him into the emergency room, and he would be taken away. The next day, I'd be allowed to visit my brother. I remember one time when he seemed to be more hose and machine than flesh. It was a terrifying sight, especially for a young kid.

These middle-of-the-night trips went on for years. I would be shocked awake and scramble to the hospital, each time outracing death. To this day, I am still startled, my heart immediately racing, when anyone tries to rouse me from sleep. What we learn as children often carries through into our adult lives.

Throughout my childhood, I was haunted by a recurring dream about my brother. In it, our class was on a school trip to the Ontario Science Centre. We explored various interactive displays on physics, sound, and animal biology. A massive transparent cylinder contained a preserved elephant heart. I made my way along the exhibits and then broke away from the other kids to follow a dark corridor. As I moved along rows of taxidermic animals and insects, I saw a lit glass tank in the middle of the hallway. It was about the size of a coffee table at counter height, allowing for a good view of what the glass cube contained. Inside was a small creature about the size of a six-year-old. I pressed my hands against the glass, and the lights illuminated to reveal my brother languishing inside. He was trying to hold his head up, lying in his yellow Winnie-the-Pooh onesie.

"Craigie!" I screamed. He was trapped in a cruel terrarium for all to view. No one seemed to notice. Mothers walked past me as I called out for help.

"Please help him," I implored. "Please do not leave him in there." No one came to his aid.

I would wake screaming from this nightmare. I would run to my brother's room to find him sleeping, and I'd sit beside his bed, placing my hand on his chest to confirm that he was breathing. I would wipe his sweaty hair from his brow and stay with him until I calmed down, knowing he was still my brother and not some scientific anomaly that entertained curious crowds.

Suddenly, I awoke in the desert from this same childhood nightmare to see what appeared to be a dark apparition floating above me, which quickly evaporated to reveal the blinding sun. It was high now, and my limbs were splayed in the sand. It was as if I were crucified, bound to the ground. I could not move. I was paralyzed.

A younger version of Craig sat cross-legged beside me in the sand. His fine, blond hair stood straight up on one side, like he had just awoken. He was wearing the same yellow Winnie-the-Pooh onesie, stained with food. He often drooled in his sleep, leaving remnants down his bib.

His appearance was as I remembered him from my young childhood. He was gaunt and spindly with unseen strength in his limbs. Everything about him looked atrophied, like pictures of prisoners of war or concentration-camp victims. Only his skull seemed full. He had one eye pointed away, but his narrow face was looking at me.

"Bus?" my brother asked.

The bus took him to his day programs, which he loved. "Bus" was one of his favorite words, along with "pizza" and "fuck." I'd taught him the latter term by repeating it when my parents left us in the back seat of the family car on a particularly hot summer day. They were inside a store, and I wanted to make them pay for abandoning us with only partly open windows. Naturally mischievous, Craig saved the f-word for special occasions to elicit a reaction. He would slur out "fuck!" and laugh at the shock on the faces of the people around him.

"Yes, Craigie, the bus is coming," I whispered. Our trip together was not finished. We had more stops to make. Like the way dreams suddenly shift location or setting, my dusty bed evaporated, and I was back in our childhood town house. I was transported back to the home where I'd spent many of my teenage years caring for Craig. My father had left us by then, and my mother worked multiple jobs to pay the bills. She worked for a construction business during the day and then went to a data-entry job at night. That left me to look after my disabled brother. As much as I loved Craig, I was losing my adolescence to responsibilities for which I was too young. My friends would go to parties, and I would stay home with him.

Craig was high needs. When I described my brother during those years, most people inferred that Craig was autistic in terms of speech and comprehension, with a palsy that limited his ability to walk. But that was only part of the picture. Craig was a childlike teen who used a wheelchair. His legs twisted at uncomfortable-looking angles, his two eyes were determined to focus on different places, and his hands were palsied, one often slapping his face as it was driven by one of his tics.

While at that point feeding was no longer a life-and-death effort, he still needed help, and he wore diapers too. Changing your teenage brother's diaper is not something anyone should have to do. He was also easily bored and mischievous. Left alone, he would find something to get into, tossing objects from their perch like a malevolent cat. I'd read him books or watch TV with him. He liked toddler programs. By then, I was interested in *The A-Team* and *Battlestar Galactica*, the *Star Wars* films, and Chuck Norris martial-arts movies. I was a teenager. I wanted action scenes and beautiful women, not the synthetic feathers of Big Bird and his imaginary sidekick, Mr. Snuffleupagus, from *Sesame Street*.

To pass the time, I sometimes tied a long rope around one of Craig's toy bears or stuffed *Sesame Street* characters, and we'd toss them out of the upstairs window onto the driveway below. He would laugh maniacally as I hoisted the toy up for another go. His laugh was infectious and would get me going too. In my mind, I was getting him back. He was just happy to spend time with his big brother. He did not care what we did, but the chaos was a bonus.

Once, I misjudged the length of the rope, and *Sesame Street*'s Ernie pendulated through the garage-door window, knocking out the pane. We hoisted Ernie back up, and my brother laughed even harder. When my mother came home, I was glad Craig's limited vocabulary prevented him from selling me out. I claimed ignorance, and she blamed "those fucking kids playing hockey" on the street in front of our house. I'd dodged another bullet, and my brother and I shared a secret, just like so many siblings do.

We made another stop. Craig rewound time, showing me the days before our father left. We were sneaking upstairs at bedtime to hide behind the living-room curtains, waiting for my mother to pass by.

"Boo!" we screamed while jumping out from our hiding place.

My mother shrieked like she had been shot, and Craig howled with delight. I took the flak for working him up before bedtime, but it was worth it, as he now showed me. Our nightly routine was his daily dose of Christmas. He loved our antics. We were not dealt a typical brotherly hand, but we were best friends, sworn enemies, and forever companions. I had long felt a kind of shame, thinking he had resented his childhood, which was marred by my disgruntled caretaking. He did not. He loved every minute. He loved me for never leaving him behind.

Eventually, though, I did just that. In my last year of high school, we moved in with my mother's new husband, Bob. He was divorced (his wife had left him years before) and seemed willing to open his home not only to my mother but also to a severely disabled thirteen-year-old. In my opinion, that was all he had going for him. We had a shell-thin relationship; perhaps it was what could only be expected between a man set in his ways and an arrogant teenager at the height of his know-it-all-ness. He was a jerk, but I was a quick-witted asshole who judged everyone through a moral lens of right and wrong that had no aperture for gray.

One night, we had an altercation over my mixtapes. I had left them beside a stereo I'd been banned from using, though of course I used it anyway. My mixtapes were now missing, and I accused my stepfather of stealing them and lying about their disappearance.

"Where are my tapes, Bob?" I accused, secure in my teenage knowledge that he was the culprit.

"Don't be ridiculous," my mother said, defending him. "He wouldn't take your tapes. He doesn't even like your music."

Our argument spilled out onto the front lawn, where we decided to settle it like men. Puffing our chests, we pushed each other, threatening blows that never came. While I do not remember what we said, it was cruel and intended to hurt.

I left the field of battle and avoided home for the remainder of the summer. Then, I went off to university and never returned home.

At the end of the first school term, my mother called.

"Mark, I think it is best if you do not come home this summer," she announced, to which I said nothing. "It is for the best. Bob is set in his ways, and you are a proud young man."

I mustered my strength and ignored the pain that pulled at the old wound that ran between us. "Fine." I deflected to camouflage my disappointment and hurt. I felt abandoned. Worse, I felt cast off. "I guess I can find an apartment here in London." At the time, I was living in a residence of the University of Western Ontario.

"I found you a place at U of T for the summer," she offered, like some inadequate olive branch. Living at the University of Toronto was geographically closer to home, which, perhaps in her mind, somehow diminished the banishment.

That was it. At eighteen, I accepted my fate, walking into the urban wilderness to find my own way. My mother needed my stepfather's help to support my brother. I was self-sufficient. It made sense—though that didn't make it feel any better. Unlike the young daughter in *Sophie's Choice*, I had not been sent to the gas chambers of a Nazi death camp. However, I still felt like the child who had been sacrificed to create a path forward for my brother.

This separation meant the end of spending significant time with my brother. I graduated from university, settled in another town, and saw Craig during the prescribed holidays. At Thanksgiving and Christmas, I would come home for the day. By then, my stepfather and I had patched things up. We had a congenial respect for each other. I valued his support of my family, and he admired my tenacity.

My skewed sense of object permanence placed my brother back in the beaker when I was away. I did not consciously think he stopped existing when I was gone, but I assumed his life was somehow less fulfilling. I did not consider that we were flowing like the two rivers of my poem, sometimes close and sometimes far apart.

Our Christmases were filled with dinner antics to make him laugh, like tossing brussels sprouts. He would erupt in hoots and do his best to chuck a green projectile back at me while the other dinner guests giggled and my mother attempted to rescue the meal's dignity. Then, our rivers would separate. In hindsight, it was no different from the paths of any siblings. In adulthood, we start new families and go our own ways, reuniting only at certain moments.

At the time of my trip into the desert, Craig had moved

into a downtown condominium with 24-7 care, had a room-
mate, and spent his days at various programs. He went sailing
on Lake Ontario and sat in the front row at the concerts and
shows at Massey Hall. He loved ABBA and singing along to
the movie version of *Mamma Mia!* The story was likely lost on
him, but the encore of ABBA hits filled his cup. He had become
a full version of himself, with a new life within his community.

"He will never forgive you for abandoning him," the manifestation of Darkness spoke.

I wept and begged for my brother's forgiveness. I had abandoned him when I went to university with barely a backward
glance. "I am sorry, brother," I sobbed. "I am sorry I abandoned
you." What had I done? "I was angry with Mom and Bob, and it
cost you." What time, experiences, mischief, connection, and
love had we lost because of my pigheaded, inflexible ego?

Craig had taught me compassion and an understanding
that what others considered different was just its own version of normal. I could forgive the world's harshness because I
knew kindness meant more than profit. He was my first love.

My brother rested his head on my heaving chest and pat-
ted my hair, cooing. This was his version of affection; he'd
croon "aah" while petting you like a dog. I remembered when
he would do the same with Bandit and then say "woof!" to her.
She would sit patiently beside him, gently holding space for
him, and I would do the same. Now, we had reversed roles, and
he was holding space for me.

Through the confusion of my desert mind, my brother
thanked me. He was not sure my banishment was necessary,
but he understood that it affected me and that I'd taken the
punch to protect him.

With that, he smacked my forehead and hollered, "Ouch!"
before he let me go. I laughed through the tears. That was
him. He was a joker. He was my Kokopelli—the southwestern Native American deity depicted with a hunched back

and playing a flute. Associated with childbirth and music, Kokopelli was above all else a trickster. I closed my eyes once more and sighed. I lay in my dirt grave, thanking him for being my brother. When I opened my eyes, he was gone. And so, too, was the darkness that had flitted and floated in my gut-wrenching memories.

—

One more story about Craig, though it happened years later, when I was in my mid-fifties and in Florida attending a conference. I had just returned to my hotel room after delivering the opening keynote when my wife called.

"Honey, Craig is in the hospital," she said with compassion.

She asked me to remain calm while she explained that Craig had suffered a stroke or cerebral event from which he would likely not recover. The doctors gave him a couple of days to live.

I arranged the next flight back to Toronto to be with him. This was the height of the COVID-19 pandemic. Passengers had to wear masks on the plane, and customs caused delays as they staggered spacing in the arrivals hall. It could delay deplaning by hours. I informed the flight crew of my brother's precarious state, who radioed ahead to the airport. An airline representative met me and escorted me through customs. From there, I had a car waiting to take me to the hospital.

When I arrived, I found him sunk into his hospital bed. He was on oxygen, and intravenous tubes fed medicine into his arms. My mother was there keeping him company. She told me he was mostly unresponsive. He had suffered an embolism, the result of a massive tumor in the occipital lobe of his brain. It would be a blessing if he passed quickly, she told me. The prognosis ruled out recovery, and death would be slow, full of hallucinations and blinding migraines.

I went to his bedside and gently stroked his hair. He turned to look at me and opened his bloodshot eyes. He smiled and grunted. "I'm here, little brother," I told him. I took his hand as he slipped back into a morphine pond. That was the last time he showed any response to the people around him.

The following day, he was transported to a palliative-care facility on a side road off Queen Street. It was a converted church that served as a home to a different kind of angel, those in the form of caregivers and doctors. Their job was to make the transition into death as comfortable as possible. They kept him on a drip feed of painkillers, put soothing drops in his drying eyes, and bathed his sweaty body. He was beyond water and food. The doctor explained that he would either die of dehydration or suffer another embolism. They kept him on medication to reduce the chance of another cerebral event.

For days, my mother and I sat with him. He lay still. I never knew if he was aware of our presence, but I hoped he was. We watched TV, and I tried to work on my laptop. Every time a nurse came to check on Craig, my mother asked them how long he would last, like they could check the train schedule and predict his departure.

"You will know," a nurse kindly explained. "The signs are unmistakable."

From that point on, my mother called a nurse every time his breathing changed.

"Nurse," she uttered, "I think his breathing is different." The nurses remained patient as I stepped in to explain.

"Mom, that's not his last breath," I gently scolded. "You will know it when you hear it." Thus, we spent our next few days at his bedside, my describing his breathing and the nurses practicing grief in the face of a grieving mother.

On his final day, I asked the doctor what could be done to speed up his passing. He explained that the antiepileptic drug could prolong his life. I instructed the doctor to cease his dosage. It was the evening of July fourth, one month shy of his fifty-first birthday. My mother and I sat watching coverage of the American celebrations in Washington, DC. The fireworks exploded in glorious colors as big bands played sycophantically patriotic tunes. A colleague sent rooftop videos of the same fireworks we saw on TV. We felt like we were there in the nation's capital. But Craig's breathing wrenched us back to the room as the fireworks came to a crescendo.

Craig's breathing became raspy and labored. He inhaled deeply, and then—nothing. I sobbed, and we held his hands. My mother cried and told him she loved him. Then, when he seemed gone, he took another rattling breath and convulsed.

My mother cried, "Oh, God, please end his suffering." I gripped his hand and simultaneously rubbed her arm. She pleaded with an unseen force. "Stop this. He cannot take anymore."

The time between each slipping breath grew, and he finally drew his last. My mother wailed like a wounded beast. I have never heard a sound so haunting as that of a mother losing her child. My heart broke for her as I struggled to accept my brother's death.

We cried and held each other.

Finally, I said, "Trust Craig to steal the show. He probably thought the fireworks were for him." We found a brief solace in my joke, though it could not remedy our sorrow. We sat with him for a while, and then, with no reason to stay, in turn we kissed his lifeless face and left.

The staff lined the front walkway, each holding a candle in Craig's honor. I thanked the workers as we passed and helped my mother up the block to my truck.

We kept my brother's ashes in a porcelain *Sesame Street* Cookie Monster jar until we buried him. It seemed the best way to honor his spirit. He loved that furry blue creature, and he loved life, one cookie at a time. *C* was for Craigie.

Craig had lived life to the fullest, regardless of his debilitating impairments. He sailed, sang from the front rows of shows, and enjoyed the little moments. His ember burned continuously throughout his life. His disabilities freed him from the limitations of normal societal obligations.

I finally gave in to my mother, who was desperate to dispose of his ashes. For the better part of a year, she planned in detail how she wanted to gather and spread his ashes in Lake Ontario, where Craig had enjoyed sailing. But it turned out that disposing of human remains in that way was illegal. Over time, she became more desperate. Behind my house was a water-management pond.

"Why don't we place him in there?" she suggested one summer evening while sitting on our deck, which overlooked the pond.

"No," I countered. "The pond is a storm pond. It is an overflow from the sewers."

"But he loved sailing on the water," my mother clamored on.

I agreed that a burial at sea was appropriate, but not in a sewer pond.

Later that year, my aunt was visiting from Scotland. With her help, we settled on spreading Craig's ashes in the Grand River, which runs through the Elora Gorge, about an hour north of our home. A Scot had settled the town in the late 1800s, and it seemed as good a place as any to lay my brother to rest. The Elora Gorge was a tourist attraction, home to restaurants and hotels. We would give him a watery burial and then eat a meal of remembrance.

On a warm summer day, my mother, aunt, wife, and I made our way to the small Wellington County town and parked on the main street near the bridge that crossed the Elora Gorge Falls. Old stone buildings spoke of a time when the town lived on trade from the flour mills powered by the river. The streets were packed with tourists. The limestone buildings, quarried from nearby rocks, had shed their history to now hock vacationers' wares. The bridge was too crowded to pull out the Cookie Monster jar and scatter ashes. Someone would find offense, and we would likely end up confronted by the police. My brother would have loved that scenario, but it wasn't something we wanted to face.

"What about that walkway behind the buildings?" I suggested. We paraded down to inspect the pathway away from the crowds. The waters along the walkway were stagnant, choked with reeds, and topped with what looked like days-old creamer on a Starbucks drink. It was putrid.

"The water is gross," I commented. "And we are behind people's apartments."

"I don't know what to do," my distraught mother cried. "I can't keep his ashes anymore."

We stood like a group of amateur criminals, building up the courage to commit our impertinent act. After several minutes of unproductive discussion, we agreed this would be the spot.

I pulled the bag of ashes from its container and handed it to my mother to go first. The longer we stood there, the angrier with her I became for choosing this spot. I thought her plan was lousy, and this only added to the travesty.

She said her goodbyes and dumped a portion of the ashes into the frothy water. The ashes did not sink. They floated like silky dust on the oily surface of the stagnant water.

"See you, Pizza Head." I whispered my nickname for him as I dumped my portion of his ashes into the river. My mother burst into tears, and my aunt held her. She sobbed and cried as I stared at his ashes, floating in this festering mess. It was done.

I was mortified. Like the water, I would fester in the feeling of resentment toward my mother for choosing that place.

I blamed her. It felt like she was checking off a box and that it did not matter how undignified the result had been. I carried that resentment for almost two years until I returned to the scene of the crime.

About the same time of year, my wife and I, with my mother, returned to Elora for dinner. We had picked roses from our garden and intended to toss them over the falls in Craig's memory.

We parked in the same spot on the street and walked to the bridge. I expected memories of his burial and my resentment to surface, but they did not. We climbed the bridge and looked down at the spot from which we had spread his ashes. The reeds and muck were gone, replaced by a boat launch. The sign above the moored canoes and kayaks read STARLIGHT AND MUSICAL CRUISES.

A place of sorrow was flushed of resentment and replaced with a business that provided what Craigie loved most: sailing and singing. My inner ember glowed. We walked over to the bridge, and I tossed my rose into the water.

"Thank you," I said to Craig, as much as I did to Source. How he had visited me in Death Valley years ago was a mystery. But this was clearly a sign that he was now in a better place.

I was finally at peace with his passing, and I could close a wound that had festered between my mother and me.

MY UNCLE

Bandit woofed a welcome as the next stranger came to me. I was delirious, but I saw my Uncle Niall in his gray trousers and blue Marks & Spencer jumper, covered in dog hair. His red beard glowed in the desert sunlight as he cast his kind eyes on my disheveled form.

I was less surprised by his arrival than I was curious about how he could wear clothes designed for the damp of Scotland, where he'd lived. The desert heat was unrelenting at its zenith. He stood as comfortably as if he were lounging on his worn settee in his living room, surrounded by his dogs.

His arrival was as impossible as Craig's. Unlike my living brother, Niall had passed away decades ago. Was he a ghost, or some friendly manifestation of Spirit here to bring me a message? My indecision drifted away, replaced by the overwhelming recognition of his absence in my life. Seeing him standing there was like looking at marks in a carpet that confirmed a past impression from a piece of heavy furniture, now gone.

"I've missed you, Niall," I cried from my bed in the desert sand.

Years before, Niall's backaches had turned to excruciating pain, and one morning, he could not move his legs to get out of bed. Testing revealed an irreversible growth on his spine.

I was still painting watercolors back then and had painted a blue-footed booby for Niall. He called it his "get-well picture." I chose the sizable seagull-like beast because he and my aunt Brenda had visited the Galapagos Islands, the home of this bird. Eventually, my paintings and the cutting-edge treatments could not stop his inevitable slide toward death.

Brenda had been destined to become a doctor. She was a competent and dedicated specialist in pediatric oncology, treating children with cancer. It seemed her reward for saving countless children was to watch cancer take her husband. But upon his diagnosis, Brenda jumped into action—this was her realm. She had access to experimental treatments, and she had a mind to save him. I always wondered if that moment was when she realized what she had with Niall. Her clinical facade crumbled to reveal a wife fighting the slide toward widowhood.

At some point, he pleaded to surrender from the unrelenting tests and treatments that transformed his body from a patient to a battlefield. Niall died, and Brenda was left a broken widow. She loved him profoundly, though she'd never been an overly affectionate person. Now, she begged for the time back to show him more frequently what he'd meant to her. At his funeral and in the years that followed, I saw my aunt openly sobbing, something very unlike her generally calm and in-control demeanor. For years, she lived submerged in sadness.

A career as a pediatric oncologist is perhaps one of the bravest vocations possible. Every day, she faced heartbreak, helping parents make unthinkable choices when it came to their sick children. Every day, she faced death. She swam in an ocean of pain and unimaginable suffering, trying to keep her head above water long enough to save one more patient. From what I could see, each loss was another drowning bairn (the Scottish word for "child"), permanently affixing their tiny hands to her ankles, pulling her toward the depths of loss.

Before Niall's death, when I was banished from my mother's home (not that Brenda knew that, and I never told her), I spent a summer living with my aunt and her husband. He was a kind man who came from money, a barrister by trade, who wore everyday clothes. He loved his dogs: Ben, a benevolent bulldozer of a yellow Labrador, and Angus, a chocolate-treat-spoiled King Charles spaniel.

Niall was the antithesis of the old-money wealth from which he came. His mother once gifted him a Mercedes for Christmas, likely because she thought his car was too pedestrian or more akin to a servant's mode of transport. The sportscar was red and flashy—the antithesis of his character. Niall never considered money as valuable as his love for his dogs, my aunt, and the time he spent at the lochs of the Scottish west coast.

I was related to Brenda by blood; she was my mother's

sister and had married Niall later in life. Though I didn't know him at all at the time, that summer, I spent more time with Niall than with Brenda. He made space for me and became my uncle within hours of meeting him. There was no "in law" needed to prefix his relation to me. He was the man I needed in my life—successful but soft. He showed me Glasgow as we talked about life and walked the dogs. My aunt was at the hospital most nights, so he and I would nip off to the curry house off Byres Road or spend an evening in a swanky restaurant suitable for the backdrop to a mafia movie.

Now, in the desert, Niall showed me his love for Brenda and reassured me that he was rewarded with her love. He knew her love language was not overt but more a telepathic transfer of adoration. He confessed he was happy with his life as he rubbed Bandit's ears.

He showed me the lonely nights Brenda spent and how she threw herself into her work. He took me to a night when I'd been living with them. I was watching their small, outdated TV with its postage-stamp-size screen that sat on a table in a room with twenty-foot ceilings. The door creaked as she came in to make her way across the wooden floor to a cabinet containing liquor and crystal glasses. She asked me if I wanted a whisky. She poured two glasses, sat beside me on the settee, and passed me a glass. We had a prescriptive conversation about our day, and I told her about what the late-night news had boasted about that day's disaster headlines.

We sat watching in silence for a while. After the better part of an hour, she turned to me and shrieked. She was startled by my presence and did not seem to remember our conversation. She chastised me for scaring her and then went back to watching television. A short while later, she made her excuses and went to bed.

I'd never brought that up again and always wondered what had been going on with her. In my vision, Niall showed me the day she'd had: another child with little prospect of seeing their next Christmas and a pleading parent willing to make any sacrifice to the pharmaceutical gods if it would spare the life of their loved one. She had been so lost in their grief and mentally searching for a medical answer to the parents' prayers that she'd been barely conscious of the world around her. Niall told me that was more the norm than the exception. She could not let go of her cases at the hospital. How could she have? Children deserve more than a moment in life to suffer from a chemical poison that only slows their death and trades time for suffering.

About six years after my vision quest, I flew to London, England, to witness Brenda becoming an Officer of the Most Excellent Order of the British Empire (OBE). The ceremony took place in Buckingham Palace and was presided over by the queen herself. Brenda received the award for her work as a pediatric oncologist and for organizing fundraising to support research into treatments. Like other recipients, she had saved countless lives.

She was allowed four guests to witness the anointment, so she had invited my mother, me, and Rebecca. We wore our Sunday best and hailed a London black taxi to the palace. As the armed guards let us in the front gates, tourists took pictures and speculated about who we might be, to gain entrance to such hallowed halls.

We surrendered our passports and phones and gathered in the grand hall. The military band struck up "God Save the Queen," and we stood. Queen Elizabeth II walked in wearing a soft-pink ensemble, surrounded by her guards. One by one, the OBE recipients bowed before her as she pinned the medal on their chests. The pomp and significance were lost on my daughter. She was too young to appreciate her courtside seats to the throne in a moment few would ever experience.

Brenda likely tossed the medal in her desk, to be lost

among paperwork, broken pens, and spilled packets of staples. She did the work and avoided the accolades. She would always remain a closed, private person.

In the stifling heat of the desert, Niall's arrival helped me to breathe. Tears ran unnoticed. I felt a pang of regret for what could have been. I ached for Niall. I craved more time with him more than I craved food, as starved as I was.

I wanted closeness with Brenda. The dreadful apparition of Darkness taunted me. "You will never be close with your aunt," it pronounced. Its declaration only heightened my awareness of my distance from relatives like her. Emigration from Scotland had robbed me of time with a clan I would never know—each relative who'd passed on obscured my hope of finding my family in thin memories and lost contact information.

I knew I was closer to Brenda in many ways than I was to my mother. Brenda and I had focused on our careers and found professional success. She had an intellectual and logical approach to life, like I did. I viewed the spiritual through the lens of science. I applied physics and logic to solve a problem that was the domain of emotion and faith.

Most of all, I wanted Brenda in my life. She had to be more than a sporadic visitor. Niall said his goodbyes and petted Bandit one last time. She wagged her tail as he said, "I will let you get on with it."

I wept in memory of a village stolen from me at a young age. "Even your aunt would not choose you," Darkness rejoiced. I wept for Brenda and her silent, unseen loss. Most of all, I wept for losing what could have been.

MY GRANDFATHER

My mother, Sandra, was a survivor. That was what Brenda, her younger sister, called her. "The one thing you can't deny about

Sandra is that she's a survivor," she would say with an air of bewilderment, if not pride.

She had survived, leaving all she knew in Aberdeen, Scotland, to sail the Atlantic to Canada. She had survived rheumatic fever. She had survived the torment and abuse of my father. She had survived parenting a severely disabled son.

My mother was also a rebel. She railed against the inherent duties of the eldest sibling. She would iron, clean, and cook, helping my grandmother while her younger sister hid, troll-like, in her room, studying. Brenda was intellectual. She was smart and excelled at school, while Sandra showed little interest in academics and gravitated to pretty dresses, makeup, and boys.

She would sneak out at night to go dancing. One night, she missed the last bus home and started walking. A policeman came upon her. He knew she was too young to be out that late and gave her a lift home in his police car, which people called "jam sandwiches" based on the orange-red stripe that ran the length of the white vehicle. He let her out just down the street from her house and watched her safely home. Somehow, she'd dodged the trouble of a police-escorted late-night return from a forbidden night out.

My mother wore her strawberry blond hair like a crown. Nights of dancing were her coronation. Along the way, she met my father, when she was seventeen and he was twenty-two. He was dark, handsome, charming, and full of life. She later told me about the time she snuck out with a group of friends and drove from Aberdeen in the northeast of Scotland to Liverpool, on the west coast of England. They saw the Beatles live at the Cavern before they became an international sensation. They were not quite yet bigger than Jesus (as John Lennon would later quip), but they were magnetic enough to draw fans from all across the United Kingdom.

My father worked as a financial clerk and spent weekends

with mates on the motor-racing circuit, camping and cavorting when they were not around race cars. He smoked his cigarettes like men did in European movies from the sixties, a cigarette dangling from their lower lip as they spoke. I always suspected my father had one more thing going for him: My grandparents—Sandra's parents—did not like him. Back then, age gaps were not criminal, but still, an older man could be dangerous. Older men had ideas and desires; my grandfather knew where that led. I will never know if my grandparents hated him then, but he certainly thought they did. He did steal away their daughter, moving her from Aberdeen to the big city of Edinburgh.

My mother could have lived a much different life if born in a different time or place. Had she been born in California, she would have followed a band around like the girls in *Almost Famous*, driving from city to city for a chance at partying with the band members. She was not a hippie. My mother was too prim for that. The free nature of the flower people of San Francisco in the sixties and seventies was their commonality.

While Vietnam raged, and souls like Sparrow Hart wept as America approached a moral crossroads, Britain was steaming into a recession and economic collapse. Job prospects for the young sank faster than ships in war convoys as inflation raced heavenward like the V-2 rockets. Especially after my arrival, my father was determined to find a new home with better prospects. British colonies like Canada and Australia held promise and escape from his ghosts, which trolled their cheap flat in Edinburgh.

My parents bundled me and a few steamer trunks onto the *Empress of Ireland*, a ship bound for North America. They crossed the unforgiving North Atlantic before arriving in the calmer water of the Saint Lawrence Seaway.

As my father worked, my mother spent her days with me.

We watched *Sesame Street* with our cat, Susie, who reluctantly kept me company during my childhood programs. When I reached school age, my mother walked me to and from. I do not remember these walks, but my next visitor showed me.

My grandfather arrived, stooping to pet Bandit. She sat up and leaned into his leg. They had never met on earth, but a bond had formed in Source, much like a solar system with me as its sun.

He stood in his gray double-breasted suit, like I had seen in pictures. Tall for a Scot and deathly lean, he was unhealthy most of his life. After serving in the South Pacific during World War II, he was gaunt, the result of malaria and malnutrition during the war.

Unlike many, he survived his tortured ordeal, fighting the Imperial Japanese forces. What came back from the war was an unhealthy husk. He had married my grandmother on leave before he departed, like so many couples had. They knew their marriage would not start in earnest until he returned from service, assuming he did. After, they made up for lost time and produced my mother and aunt.

He never spoke of the war. His gentle, soft-spoken nature was no match for the horrors he had witnessed. Rather than engage with my grandmother's antagonistic nattering, he would turn down his hearing aids and ignore her.

The night he died, he'd appeared at the foot of my bed and wordlessly said his goodbyes. Now, he was here in the desert with me.

Unlike Niall or Craig, my grandfather spoke without words. He told me that my mother loved me and that he'd wanted more for my mother. Brenda had studied medicine, while my mother had shown little academic interest but was feisty enough to make it independently.

He'd never trusted my father, who would often avoid direct eye contact when discussing serious subjects. My grandfather feared that my father would abandon his family when times were tough. Perhaps the war had honed his ability to recognize those who stayed with comrades and those who ran from conflict.

While he was alive, he never knew of the domestic abuse in which his daughter and grandchildren lived. Our screams could not make their way across the Atlantic to Scotland to be heard with his hearing aids. Even if he suspected my father was abusive, he could not have imagined the full extent. He silently wept and asked my forgiveness. Had he known, he would have acted. He recounted the time my parents were boarding the ship to sail to Canada.

"If you ever need to come home, we will pay for a ticket," he said to my young mother. "But we're not buying a ticket for *him*." He glanced at my father.

He knew in that moment that whatever relationship he and my father may have had, it had been torpedoed by those words. Whether my father heard him or not, the sentiment was palpable. I knew my grandfather had wanted the best for us, and he was scared to lose his daughter. He did not want his family across an ocean. He was a simple man and had seen death and loss during the war. He did not want to lose anyone else. And after all, my grandfather's concern, or intuition, was right. What was to come for his loved ones was worse than he feared.

As dreams shifted effortlessly from one scene to another, we faded into Christmas in Canada. I was a young teenager. My father had left us. My mother came home from work carrying large shopping parcels. A decorative paper shopping bag toppled against the wall as she removed her coat and boots. I could see the hardcover books inside. She had purchased Dungeons & Dragons guides. She had gone to a unique store in downtown Toronto, far out of her way, to find them. I loved her for it. She had chosen me. I had the two books already, but it was the thought that mattered. That gesture meant the world to me.

I felt my spiritual dog shift her weight from one hip to the other, and she lay back down, placing her head on my belly. She sighed with the effort, and I sank into a stupor of memories as my grandfather showed me the time my mother chose me over food.

My mother was heading out the door to work, and I was tagging along, pleading for some money to go to the department store and buy a *Star Wars* toy. *The Empire Strikes Back* was in theaters, launching a new torrent of toys and memorabilia. I was tired of my patchwork LEGO vehicles and wanted something novel to pass the time. I argued my side as she countered with reasonable facts about money and how much things cost.

"Things are expensive, and your father doesn't give me a cent." We had no money beyond what would pay the bills, but I didn't understand that.

"Look," I said, opening her wallet to find a twenty-dollar bill. "You have money." She was late for work and gave in to my juvenile greed. I kept the money, and she walked out the door to face a day and evening of work across two jobs with no money to eat.

My adult self understood the sacrifice she'd made to please her child. I understood how twenty dollars was worth more to her than its face value. She could have used it for more than a plastic toy with a short shelf life that would soon be added to a heap of retired playthings.

I wept again, appreciating through an adult lens how terrifying it must have been to be alone with two children, one of whom had special needs. I had no idea how close we'd come to eviction, dancing from one debt to the next. She'd shielded me from that.

My grandfather was showing me how my mother had

loved me and cared for me, even when it seemed she was focused only on Craig. Her "favoritism" had been born out of necessity. She had not intentionally chosen my brother over me; it happened in easily justified increments. It was not so much a choice as a slow-building outcome.

My grandfather showed me the hours and hours my mother had fought and pleaded with government officials to establish programs for people like my brother. We were the voyeurs of the tireless meetings, bickering, and struggles my mother endured to get someone to listen.

But my mother's work led to the formation of two foundations for disabled adults. She rallied a clan of parents with similar support needs and established the first foundation by building a fund to purchase housing and to staff the homes with round-the-clock support for disabled adults. The second created a day program to keep people like my brother from spending their days staring out windows and drooling. Her legacy meant that Craig and others like him experienced a dignified and fulfilling life.

In this respect, my grandfather was right. My mother was a marvel. She was a survivor who found strength when others drowned. But other less favorable memories arose. My grandfather seemed to turn off his hearing aids and ignore the times my mother should have chosen differently. "It's not that simple," I shouted at my grandfather. I thought of Craig and how he had needed her full attention. I could accept that, even if it meant I didn't always get what I wanted or thought I deserved. He was my brother, and I was mature enough to understand he needed more of her time and care than I did. But it still hurt sometimes when I wanted the space to be a child, a human being, and the weight of her expectations and criticism came down on me.

Another day from our childhood formed around my grandfather and me. We watched as my mother helped my brother leave the garage. I was carrying the grocery bags and impatiently pulled the garage door closed. It clocked my brother in the head as it swung on cranky springs. I had misjudged their pace and used too much force to swing the door, and it cut my brother across the forehead. In an instant, my impatience turned to remorse.

"Oh, shit. I'm sorry!" I yelled.

My mother turned and snapped, "You're just like your father—you don't care who you hurt!"

With that, she helped my brother inside and left me there to feel the sting of her words. They hit me like a punch in the gut. The force penetrated my soul and robbed me of any sense of worth. I knew who my father was, and to be his little doppelgänger stole my confidence. Was I him? Like my father, would I hurt those I loved and abandon them when things got hard? I was no longer sure.

We watched the younger me, left behind on the driveway, fight back his tears. My grandfather placed his hand on my shoulder in reassurance. *She didn't mean it,* his gesture seemed to say. She was angry and startled, lashing out with the closest object: her anger at my father. We stood there, watching my little self gather his wits before heading inside to apologize.

We were back in the desert now.

Like my mother, I struck out with what was close at hand. "Where were you?" I shouted. "Did you know what was happening? My father was a monster. Why didn't you do anything?" I stared at my grandfather's calm face.

He spoke wordlessly. "We did not know." I understood what I heard in my head. His lips never moved. His face showed remorse. They might have suspected but never knew the extent. I felt as much as I knew that they would have moved heaven and earth to help us, had they known what was happening.

My grandparents were aware of my parents' financial troubles, and they had lent us money when we were desperate. He showed me a time when they'd visited us in Toronto before my parents separated, and they'd made time to sequester my mother to ask what was going on. My mother never revealed the true extent of our suffering at the hands of my father. She never talked about the hair pulling and wrestling on the stairs. She never admitted the extent of the violence.

I stumbled back from the revelation that my parents hid the facts from my grandparents. Rescue was near and ready to swoop in, and yet we had to tread water in destitution with the violence of my father hanging around our necks like the proverbial albatross.

My grandfather regretted his inaction and would have done anything within his power to help us.

We stood looking at each other. My anger with my mother was boiling up with the growing desert heat. Had she kept the domestic savagery secret out of pride? Was it that simple?

"Your mother will choose you, but you will never choose her now," Darkness boasted from the periphery.

My grandfather looked at me and raised his hand in a gesture of farewell. His time was limited, I understood. He faded into the desert, leaving behind an eddy of sand.

"I miss you," I called after him, but it was too late. I thought about how I had never really known him, before I faded into a restless trance.

My grandfather's visit left me with as many questions as answers. Had my mother chosen pride over safety? Was she too ashamed to admit that all those years back, she'd started down a path that would lead to suffering, pain, and remorse? I would never truly know why she had not sought help.

Did she even know the truth? Things were different in the 1980s. Returning to Scotland would have meant complete upheaval for all of us.

"She will never deliver you contrition," Darkness commented.

I swam in the regret of a mother making impossible choices as she simply tried to survive from one day to the next. Victims of domestic abuse often suffer in silence for fear of retaliation or destitution. Society in the seventies and eighties created patriarchal barbed wire that entrapped women in their prison of abuse. I was as much confused as I was angry.

I could not find my answers about my mother—at least not all of them. Perhaps another visitor would reveal more of the picture I could not form.

MY FATHER

I lay pressed into the ground. Darkness stood over me.

"Your father never loved you," it gloated. "He was incapable of love. It's no wonder your attempts to seek his love failed." I could feel the force relishing my anguish.

I felt the pressure on my chest abate, and I tried to sit up to see what had drawn Bandit's attention. My father was there, staring down at me.

He wore typical trousers and an unbuttoned shirt, open uncomfortably low to expose his mahogany-tanned chest. He had Black Irish blood in his veins, a blend of Portuguese, Mediterranean, and Celtic ancestry that produced the airy figure of the Irish with the black hair and sun-kissed skin of a warm-water fisherman.

I was never sure how much of his story was accurate, how much was embellished on some foundation of truth, and how much was fabricated. Separated from my Scottish roots, I have lost touch with those people who could assemble the puzzle pieces to discern the picture. A few misplaced threads among the tapestry neither changed the overall image nor disguised the blemished wall it covered.

My father had been a little boy robbed of his mother at a

young age and unloved by his stepmother. He grew up playing in the bomb craters of World War II and never knew proper nourishment, both in terms of his body and of his soul. He had lost his teeth at a young age and wore dentures most of his life. His plastic teeth produced a perfect smile that aided his charm and hid the truth of what was behind his words.

Spiritually, he was a boy stuck in the south shield, similar to me, though we'd dealt with it in different ways. He had no trust; his innocence was stolen at a young age. He was an abuser, born of the abuse he'd suffered. His past did not pardon his life's choices; it simply commuted his sentence and helped explain his abhorrent behavior. In that way, he was paroled, freed to make bad choice after bad choice. Someone else had started knocking over the row of his dominoes, but he encouraged their falling, blowing alcohol-tainted breath on each tile to ensure that it struck the next. He was determined to demolish his life.

Alcohol and smoking were excesses brought on by continual wasted potential and shame. He could blame the smoking on his generation, but not the booze. The alcohol was to numb the pain and banish the memories of repeatedly beating and cheating on my mother, and countless other shameful acts that I never knew of, though I was one of the closest people to him in life. Fears from his youth diminished his intelligence and charm. He lacked the necessary confidence and sought acceptance in the wrong place from the wrong people. He took out his life's frustrations on the wrong people.

Even after my parents divorced sometime in my teens, I sought to keep a relationship with my father while attempting to compartmentalize the cruelty I had experienced from him and the resulting shame I felt about him. For years, I would take the first step to help him and keep in contact. Most of the time, I made the effort for myself. Sometimes I did it for him. Other times, I felt I had no alternative.

One night, he assaulted his live-in girlfriend, a French Canadian mother of two little boys. He got drunk, she got belligerent, and the result was a pushing match ended by the arrival of the local police.

The next day, I drove three hours to bail him out of jail. Sometime later, I sat in court beside him while he pleaded no contest. The judge was lenient and let him off with a warning. It seemed a slap on the wrist, like a judicial version of "boys will be boys." The wheels of justice made an excuse for abuse and ushered him on to his next set of bad choices.

Another time, I went to meet him at the car dealership, where he was to return his leased Mercury Cougar after failing to make the payments. The car was his pride, and it was being repossessed. His paychecks (from a job one of his last remaining friends had found for him) could not even cover the money he'd spent on a stripper half his age.

His ego, or need to buy self-worth, was too costly. Sex and youthful flesh could not replace love and the longevity of family, and he always felt empty, looking for more.

I sat in my car that cold Saturday morning, waiting for him to pull into the dealership. I do not remember how long I waited, but it was long enough to know he was not showing up. I was angry but not surprised, so I started calling his phone. After numerous tries, he finally answered,

"Hel-lo," he slurred, as if deep asleep. He was shit-faced again, I thought. He intended to drunkenly stumble his way through this next milestone of humiliation. He would pass out while a repo company took the car from his driveway. Once again, he would run from the results of his bad choices.

"Dad, where are you?" I asked, not letting the disappointment mar my words. "You are supposed to meet me in Toronto." As I spoke to him with a tone of parental disappointment, I realized something was wrong. "Dad, what is going on?" I asked with more concern.

He was not slurring or making his usual excuses. He did not make sense. He was barely coherent.

"Are you okay?" Now my tone expressed near panic. "How much did you drink?" I asked.

Through unintelligible mumbling, I pieced together a morning of wine, whisky, and a bottle of aspirin.

He was hoping to fall asleep and not wake up. Losing the car was his breaking point in a series of self-inflicted breaking points.

"I am going to call an ambulance. I will call you right back," I told him and then hung up.

I dialed 911 and explained the situation to the operator. "No, no, he lives in Windsor," I tried to clarify. The operator seemed confused. "I am in Toronto. He was supposed to meet me. He didn't show up. I just called him, and he is sick. There is something very wrong. I think he overdosed on something."

I stayed on the phone with the 911 operator until the ambulance crew arrived at his apartment, hundreds of miles away. He went to the hospital to have his stomach pumped before rehab and then counseling to help him understand what drove him to attempt suicide.

I took the train to Windsor, Ontario, to visit him. He had the enthusiasm of a newly landed immigrant in the land of opportunity. He felt he had received some magic remedy or that someone had waved a wand and fixed his life. I knew the truth. This was a temporary pause in his cycle of addiction, self-loathing, and perpetual bad decisions.

We talked, and I wondered if I had done the right thing. Had I prolonged his suffering? Had I missed my opportunity to escape the role as his surrogate loving parent? I felt guilty about my dark and selfish thoughts.

It would not be the only time I pondered if any early demise would suit him. I sometimes wished he had died in that hospital hallway while neglected by the medical staff. They should have let him die from his brain tumors rather than stretching out his life, resigning him to more nausea, pain, remorse, and shame. His wilting body had imprisoned his mind and sentenced him to revisit his past.

I was back in the desert with my beloved dog at my side. Her tail was held in a cautious pose as she looked at my father. I looked up at him, and he smiled.

Suddenly, I was a little boy, playing with my Hot Wheels cars on the sands of Mosport (now called Canadian Tire Motorsport Park), a motorsport circuit a couple of hours east from where we lived. The circuit had fallen into disrepair after the Canadian Grand Prix had been wrestled to Montreal. It remained the playground of my youth.

He'd woken me early in the morning that day. I slept in the car as he drove to the track, and we watched the race cars at corner two as they flew over a blind crest and soared around the curves like eagles diving and climbing over an asphalt river. As a young kid, I kept myself busy playing with my toy cars, driving them around a hand-carved track that followed the ebb and flow of the sand, next to the rusted fence that separated spectators from the real track.

The smell of his aftershave, cigarette smoke, and stale beer wafted over me. Despite its rank temperance, these were good times with my father. Sometimes, at home, he would wake me late at night when our favorite movies came on TV. Back then, you scoured the weekly TV guide in the Saturday newspaper to highlight the shows and movies you did not want to miss. Reflecting the seasons, the networks seemed to show specific films around the same time of year. We would stay up to watch classic war movies like *Where Eagles Dare*, *Force 10 from Navarone*, *Battle of Britain*, and *The Dam Busters*. My favorite season was the week of James Bond films, played in order from Sean Connery's *Dr. No* through the latest Roger Moore installment.

I remembered going to drive-in movies too. My brother and I would pretend to be asleep in the back seat so my parents wouldn't have to pay for us. I would stay up to cheer on Bond as he fought millionaire narcissists in movies like *The Spy Who Loved Me* or *Moonraker*. Those good times stood out against a desert of prickly plants and animals that would snap unprovoked in this wasteland that only hurt that which it loved.

Without words, he showed me his shame. It was his Sisyphean boulder.

When he withdrew from me, it was driven by remorse. He had become the antagonist after a childhood of lovelessness and physical punishment. In his youth, children were to be seen and not heard. Transgressions were rewarded with a crisp slap or the father's belt.

Adults took sides over their children. A headmaster's report of misbehavior or academic inadequacies would ensure further corporal punishment at home. Fatherly "love" was a subscription delivered through toughness. Mothers would fret in the background and clean up the tears with assurances that the man in the child's life indeed loved them, even if their actions demonstrated something contrary. He'd continued that cycle of abuse and violence.

"I'm sorry, son." He pleaded for my understanding.

I did not understand. It was a matter of perspective and relation. He was the victim of his aggressors, yet he was the antagonist in my life. He embodied the spectral recognition that parents teach us more about what we aspire to be and less about what we want to become. His frustration had fueled his impatient fists. In response, I had become a pugilist who fought with words. I never felt the impulse to physical conflict, no matter how angry. I knew that striking another, especially a loved one, would only drive them away, not lead to understanding. Violence sowed mistrust. The recipient would walk in perpetual fear of the next time the abuser lashed out. Fear is no basis for honest communication or love. It is not a place to raise children.

In his remorse, I faced my judgment. Staring at this apparition, I understood that compassion allows us to understand before differences lead to aggression. It means not seeing the fear in others and exploiting it. Cruelty is not self-defense. It is an easy way out that robs us of the chance to reconcile.

Like my father, I was pushing away loved ones. Not physically, but my actions were born of fear nonetheless.

My father had always sought the easy way out instead of vanquishing his fears. He lied about completing his accounting degree rather than facing the risk of failing the exam. He drowned his ghosts with spirits. One by one, he cashed in the chips of friendship until whisky was the only thing that could tolerate his presence.

My father taught me what I did not want to be. I saw his cowardice for what it was, and I saw his diminished life as squandered potential.

He explained that he had been watching me from wherever he was. He was a voyeur relegated to watching but never participating. He was proud of me; I felt that. I had become the man he had not.

I shivered, thinking of the difficulties I would face when I returned from the desert. He said he was confident of my success. It was a sincere statement from him that I believed, and this time, I didn't worry about him pulling the carpet out from under my life.

But still, the good memories and this too-little, too-late pride were like islands lost in a sea of suffering. I could not forget his cruelty. I could not forgive his waste of potential.

"You're not so different from your father," Darkness spoke from all around me. "Let me show you."

CHAPTER SEVEN

The Recurring Nightmare

Death Valley, California, Day 8, Still in the Darkness

As I lay in the sand, exhausted from my last visitor, I begged Darkness for respite.

"Enough," I strained out. "No more—please." Bandit whined somewhere near me. Her pleas seemed to come from beyond a veil. I felt like I was floating in blackness, devoid of gravity or light with which to orient. I was suspended as if in the talons of a spectral raptor.

I slipped into a restless form of sleep as I lost sight of even Darkness.

When I was a child, I had a recurring feverish nightmare of walking through a dark lumberyard. As I made my way into the factory buildings, I could smell the damp sawdust and feel the chill of the evening air. The building was old and constructed of corrugated metal and rotting wood beams, like a skeletal rib cage, covered in torn, mummified flesh. The walls leaked light from the outside, creating a piano keyboard of alternating dark and light areas. The cacophony of the towering machines inside was deafening. A little girl singing drew me in, and I moved through the alleyways of conveyor belts and gnashing cutters and grinders.

This dream's landscape was beyond the reach of the laws of physics. I could hear her peaceful tune slipping between the earsplitting industrial crashes. I saw her playing on top of one of the long conveyor lines. She wore a white lace dress, like the kind often worn by young, archetypally innocent girls in movies like *The Sound of Music*. I climbed the cold metal stairs toward her, each step a jagged, toothy maw ready to strip my feet of flesh.

On an unstable catwalk, she sat at a small wooden child's table, conducting a tea party with a stuffed bear. She sang and hummed her tune as she poured tea into delicate china cups and sipped, oblivious to her strange surroundings. She sat at the junction of two massive machines, each driving a gigantic tree trunk right toward her.

No matter how much I screamed, waved, or tried to get her attention, she did not notice. The giant logs moved along their tracks toward her. She continued with her faux tea party. I screamed and waved again, to no effect.

Something grabbed me from behind and threw me from the gantry. I landed hard on the ground. My knee was soaked from the puddle in which I fell. I screamed out in pain and terror, and Darkness bellowed at me like a deranged creature.

I ran in fear, abandoning the little girl to her fate. I could not save her. It did not matter; a primal survival instinct drove me to try to save myself. I ran down the metal stairs to escape my shadowy pursuer. The nebulous creature grabbed my shoulder as I turned and ran down the next flight of stairs. I screamed and jumped from the top of the stairs.

More than once after this dream, I awoke with my mother and father standing over me. I was still screaming. My hair was tacked to my forehead, glued by the sweat from a torrid fever. My mother tried to soothe me as their dinner guests stared in horror. I was lying at the bottom of our stairs, sprawled in our living room. The factory faded away, but the girl's singing remained. As my father carried me back upstairs to my bed, I should have felt safe. But I knew I was not. I knew what would come. It was a temporary respite from the monster that would inevitably catch up to me.

My parents entertaining friends with music and wine was the opening act. Sometime during the delightful evening, my mother would say something my father took as an insult or a put-down, and he would cling to those words, sharpening them like talons. As they cleaned up the night's debris, he would lash out and start an argument, playing to a crescendo up the stairs I had run down earlier.

I woke, disturbed by raised voices and the sounds of smashing dishes. At eight years old, I lay in bed and, like a sports commentator, attempted to convince myself that everything was all right and another fight was not brewing. Their fights started like a thunderstorm. Distant rumbles of thunder made their way closer. I would pray the storm had passed, but the lightning strikes increased in frequency and loudness, confirming that the storm was rolling in. The walls shook, and I knew the storm was overhead.

My brother woke up in his room, next to mine. I ran in and tried to calm him. My parents were downstairs circling each other, looking for an opening to strike. There I sat, trying to pacify my brother as I waited for the storm to abate, which it never did. As it had countless times before, it had gathered too much energy to diffuse.

My mother screamed, and the bed shook as someone fell hard against a wall downstairs. I leaped from my bed. I was no longer the commentator; I would assume the role of referee. I ran down the stairs to find my parents locked in a duel like two rams locking horns on a cliffside.

My mother yelled, "Go back to sleep." She held on to my father's arms to prevent his strike. "Everything is okay." Her words were in stark contrast to her precarious situation.

My father's eyes were alight with loathing as his words spat like acid from his mouth. He had drowned in an alcoholic pool of self-loathing and emerged this primordial beast, fueled by every past insult and shortcoming. In his fugue, my mother assumed the role of his archnemesis, imagined to be responsible for every loss and shameful moment he had suffered.

I launched myself into the fray and grabbed at them, pleading for them to stop. "Please, Dad. Stop!" I begged. Oblivious, he threw another punch, followed by some vague accusation of infidelity. My mother responded with an insult of her own, only fueling my father's rage.

"Mom, stop!" I urged. "Stop, or he'll hurt you more—you're only making it worse!" I was ashamed that I was labeling her as the implicit aggressor.

The memories of these fights landed a one-two punch of fear and anger as I lay on the desert ground. Bandit whined and paced as I writhed, kicking up dust. I do not remember exactly how the fights ended. Sometimes, my cajoling would sink in as the booze in my father's blood waned. My parents would retreat to their corners and lick their wounds, and my mother would walk me back to bed. My mother would stay and calm me down. She would promise me that everything would be okay. The storm had passed.

But another was sure to come in its wake.

The following day, the house was a wreck. Sometimes it was random items strewn about, a dining-room chair knocked over and lights left on. I'd wake on mornings like those, wondering if he had finally killed her yet knowing I would have to wait until they rose to find out.

My brother stirred; I helped him out of bed and downstairs to make breakfast. We watched cartoons and waited for our parents to come downstairs. The echoes of the previous night rattled me, but I told myself, *Today will be fine.* We were safe until my mother came home late from work, spent too much on Christmas gifts, or shot a barb at him in front of company, stirring the next tempest. Any excuse would do for him to lash out. Living like that was like living through a year-round hurricane season.

The fighting continued through my youth. It ended in my teens when I stood up to my father. My parents were in the front hall, and the storm was brewing. By then, I was taller than he was. I summoned my strength to become a player, resigning my role as referee.

My father stepped toward my mother.

"Don't," I commanded, as much an interrogative as an imperative. I watched as the flames behind his eyes glowed brighter. I could feel the heat of his anger. My word was enough to give him pause.

"If you do, I am going to stop you," I explained, trying to hide my fear. The feeling in those moments is palpable. It is a flushing sensation that comes up from your core, accompanied by a chill that runs down your back to your toes. It is an acknowledgment of the inevitable strife about to occur, mixed with a limbic drive to overcome and survive. It is primordial. The adrenaline was doing its job, fueling my resolve.

I calmly described how I would overpower and restrain him before calling the police. He took a step toward me with eyes full of flames. Then something happened. He stepped back.

"See what you have done?" he questioned, accusing my

mother of turning me against him, before storming out of the house.

God knew where he went. All I knew was that he was not coming back. Soon after, they divorced.

After some time, I tried to build a different relationship with my father. I would scour the ashes and debris of our tornado-shattered life for some remnants of love, like a family photo or heirloom pulled from the wreckage of a killer storm. My mother resented my attempts to reconcile with him. She felt he did not deserve it. He didn't deserve his children. I guess I tried to do the same thing she did, staying in Canada instead of running back to Scotland. I was trying to salvage some vestige of fatherly love.

Nonetheless, my father lost his children. He had pushed my innocence and trust off a cliff to establish dominance over my confidence. My brother's impaired memory left little room for a father he saw once or twice in the following decade. I remember my father visiting Craig in the hospital after surgery to repair a broken hip. Craig's legs twisted beyond the limits of standard biological mechanics, and the bone had finally snapped. My brother lay in a hospital bed as my father tried to rekindle their relationship. To Craig, he was less welcome than the nurses and doctors who brought his injections and conducted painful examinations.

In the desert, my brother's spirit had told me he had not been the one to come to my father on his deathbed. My brother chose the other path and dissolved his connection to our father. I could not blame him. I cried for the loss anyway. Craig jettisoned our father because his only memories of him involved me preventing our father from killing us. Craig showed me he had no good memories from which he could rekindle a relationship.

In contrast, my father had been good to my daughter, Rebecca, in her early years. We would visit him at his shack of a cottage on Lake Huron. At one time, it was the town's general store. Now, it was a moss-covered wreck, hidden among the evergreens, a stone's throw from the lake. The cottage belonged to his second wife's mother-in-law. She was an old Italian lady who liked her naps, cooked a mean Bolognese, and looked forward to the bottle of sambuca (it had to be black) I always brought her as thanks.

Her late husband had purchased the cottage. A military flagpole stood proudly in the backyard. It flew the colors of Canada and his native Italy. He was a retired air force fighter pilot who spent time on NATO assignments in Canada. He fell in love with the land and settled there after his service. My father had added the gold and red of the Scottish Lion Rampant beside the reds and greens of Canada and Italy, and he always raised the flags while in residence and lowered the colors as the last act before departing.

Rebecca, five years old then, marched to the flagpole and helped my father ceremoniously raise the colors. We spent summer days playing under those flags overlooking our merriment. We set up a mock minigolf course using sticks and cups, and we played rounds, interrupted when Bandit would chase a rolling ball and run off with her prize. The rule was that the spot where Bandit left the ball was where you had to play from. No mulligans given.

These were memories that helped Rebecca form an admiration for her grandfather. By then, he was older and gentler, at least the side he showed her. It was not until years after my wilderness quest, as Rebecca matured, that the truth blew in, the way a wind makes its way through the gaps in cottage walls. It was the cold truth, one that troubled her. That loving, gentle figure of her childhood could not have been the same man who had beaten his wife and children before leaving them to fend for themselves. How could she reconcile her loving experience with the monster I had survived?

The truth came to her in gusts of paradoxes as she tried to piece together a bigger picture of her grandfather. She asked why I had kept a relationship with him. He was a "bad man," she reasoned, who did not deserve my love. She was not wrong. But like most things in life, it was more complicated. He was my father. The movies and motor racing were the flags I hoisted to remember the good times. I explained that his life had not been easy, and that many of my childhood experiences contributed to a wasted life. It was a half answer and a partial truth.

Your parents are connected to you, no matter how poorly they treat you. Even absent parents leave a role model–shaped hole in your life, whether their absence results from choice or ugly fate. Rebecca was analytical like Brenda and did not understand. Both her parents were loving to her, if not to each other.

"There is a bond between you and your parents deeper than time spent together. It is at the cellular level," I reasoned with her. "It is more than imprinted in your DNA; it is a bond of some force we cannot explain. It has a persistence that's stronger than gravity." I used scientific terms in the hopes of winning my case. "Think of it like quantum physics and spooky entanglement. Two subatomic particles, billions of miles apart, respond to each other. If one is negative, an electron, the other must become a positively charged proton."

She stared at me, unconvinced.

"Schrödinger's cat?"

No response.

"Okay, then what about twins, miles apart, who know the other twin is hurt?" She lit up in recognition and told a similar story of some show she had watched. "It is like that," I said. We would leave it there for now.

In time, she would understand what I was saying. I only hoped it did not take my absence to bring her to enlightenment. But in the desert, I was having doubts.

"Your mother was right," Darkness whispered. "You are like your father." The words wisped around like small eddies in the sand. "Like him, you will lose your child." Darkness's words boomed through my mind.

In the vision before me, I watched as I lost Rebecca through a train of possible scenarios. She rebelled in her teens, and some junkie stole her from me. I cringed, unable to stop the imagined inevitable. She died in a car crash, begging for her father as life seeped out of her. I screamed in agony. She disappeared, and I never knew her fate, imagining horrible scenarios. I begged Darkness to stop filling my head with excruciating visions.

The scenarios settled into a coin toss. If I left her mother, Rebecca would never forgive me, amplified by a river of vileness from my ex-wife. The other toss: I stayed with her mother until Rebecca went to university. I would pretend to be happy until the time when parental separation had less of an impact on my daughter's daily life.

I recalled a young person I'll call Emma who worked for me years ago. Her father had a similar dilemma and took the path of deferral. He waited until his kids moved out before leaving his wife and living as his true self. His best friend had been more than just a guy he hung out with over beer and sports. Their camping trips were not about canoeing and hiking at all. He was gay. He finally came out to his family when Emma was in her early twenties. She felt betrayed. His attempt to shelter her had only created a cocoon of deception. She never forgave him or spoke to him again and went so far as to change her surname to strip all remnants of their connection.

Emma's father had chosen to live a life of fraud to preserve his family. He had done it for a good reason, not wanting his children to grow up in a broken home. Yet his well-intended facade left his children feeling betrayed. Perhaps they could have handled the truth. Alternatively, maybe they resented the sacrifice. Either way, his relationship with his daughter was severed by his choice.

Similar to Emma's father, I was living a false narrative to protect my daughter. Or so I thought. If I dropped the facade and left my wife, would that alienate Rebecca? Neither seemed a guaranteed option. Each seemed to end in loss. In my dream state, I tossed my coin. Heads, Darkness wins; tails, I lose.

"Your daughter will leave you," Darkness spoke. Bandit's hackles rose, and she growled. Her head hung low, yet her eyes were steady on my unseen adversary. I wept for the loss of my daughter.

"No, I am not my father!" I refuted. "My father was undeserving, but I made the effort."

"She will not make the effort like you did," Darkness replied. "Give her up." Its demand was a dagger in my chest. I begged Darkness to convince Rebecca to forgive me, no matter which choice I made. Bandit slowly rose to her feet, low, ready to pounce.

"The price is too high; I love her too much. I will always be loving and nurturing to her. I will always be there," I cried. Whether my father was deserving or not, I made the effort to maintain a relationship. This was different from my childhood experience. Darkness was using a distorted echo to amplify my fears.

My life might have had parallels to my father's, but we were not on the same trajectory. Our lives and relationships did not have to end the same way.

"I grant the power you have over me. I recognize how you have used my fears against me," I said. I was shaking and beyond despair. Darkness savored my torment.

"I married Rebecca's mother because I was afraid no one would choose me," I admitted.

Bandit kept her gaze fixed on Darkness. She whined her concern.

I found the strength to continue. "I stayed married because I was afraid of losing my daughter." My confession eased my fear. I was not my father. I was not condemned to a similar fate.

"Darkness, I offer you this." I paused to gather my thoughts into a cohesive plan that I could agree to and deliver. "When Rebecca and I sit around a fire, we shall acknowledge how easy it is to drift from each other." Bandit relaxed her vigil. "And on the winter solstice, I will honor your place in the universe as equally important to that of light."

"Go on," Darkness commanded from all around me.

"I will place an unlit candle in the snow, as a ceremony in your name. I will meditate on the importance of balance and darkness and shadow in our lives."

The pall around my fever dream lifted. The sins of my father were not mine. I had not abandoned my brother. And most of all, life was full of difficult and potentially costly choices. My mother made hers. I would make mine.

I stroked Bandit's side, then collapsed into a dreamless sleep.

PART THREE

Return

CHAPTER EIGHT

Return of the Light

Death Valley, California, Day 8, After the Darkness

The fever broke, and my visions gave way to a consciousness resistant to the awareness that the sun was low and
light would fade soon. I no longer feared Darkness. I shifted
my legs slowly, testing the weakening bonds of the paraly-
sis that had contained my attention to my dark visitors. My
head pounded and my throat burned, preventing me from
swallowing.

My solo time was coming to an end. I dragged myself to
my water supply and labored to open a water bottle. I drank
deeply, the cool liquid dribbling down my chin and shirt. The
rivulets were a cold trail, cutting through the greasy residue of
sweat and dust. I shivered and tried to swallow, swooping my

head like a pelican extending its neck to swallow a whole fish. My throat was raw, and the cool water helped.

Had my family actually visited me? Were they still here? What had I experienced in my fever? This was not what Sparrow Hart had described. His interpretation was more like an introspective bargaining with one's depression, anger, or regrets.

I had spoken to a living brother and communed with kin who long ago passed through the veil that separates the living from the dead. The fever was gone, but the memories remained. My thoughts spun, orbiting my inner ember, which glowed like the star at the center of my spiritual solar system.

I had little time to consolidate my experience with the darkness or process all the lessons. I decided to make some notes. As I scribbled words I only partially understood, I felt like I had forgotten something. Something was missing.

I was alone.

Something more than the light of day had left. Small pebbles and dust slid down the side of the large rock that formed one side of my camp. I looked around. Nothing was there, but I was certain something had been.

"Bandit?" I called from somewhere in my subconscious. Where was she? In a flood of memories, coming too fast to capture, I saw a snippet of her lying at my side, as I flailed, prostrate in the sand. She was my guardian, and now she was gone.

"Thank you, my old friend," I said quietly.

She was gone. Again, it was a loss, just like the day I took her for her final visit to the veterinarian. "I miss you, girl," I whispered. Her absence shot like a shiver down my spine.

I was growing cold but knew I needed to focus on other things. It was my last solo night in Death Valley. Before I walked out, I had one more ceremony to complete.

The sun was dipping behind the western mountains,

reducing my time to prepare for the evening ceremony. I opened my pack, lying sideways in the dirt, and fished for my headlamp. I slid it over my head and draped it around my neck. I would need it soon.

Tonight, I was to sit vigil all night as part of a ceremony to find my purpose. I would pray and meditate, asking the spirits for a sign or a bearing to direct me. I gathered the stones that formed my bed space and rearranged them into a circle large enough in which to sit cross-legged. I created two perpendicular rows of rocks to transect the circle into quadrants. I first took a bearing from my compass to align the rows to the cardinal directions. At the points of the wheel, I placed quartz stones to denote the directions.

As I constructed my circle, memories from the darkness came back in waves. The first waves lifted and then dropped me like a bobbing flotsam. Over time, the cycle eroded, and the waves and troughs slowed in frequency and amplitude. The undulations eased, and my karmic seasickness abated.

I surveyed my circle. It was in reach of my altar, which faced east. I was ready for the evening. I spent some time preparing for my departure the following morning by packing my tarps and sleeping bags into their compartments in my backpack. I placed a fresh candle in my lantern and then turned my attention to my trash pile, collecting shavings from my drawing pencils and crushing each empty water bottle into a small disk. All that was left to do in the morning would be to scatter the stones, disassemble my altar, and make my way down the butte for the last time.

As the sun set, I gave up on the notion of creating a fire. I was too tired to wander around collecting scrub, as I had cleaned out most of the proximal burnable material. Besides, I had faced my inner darkness; I could face something as simple as the night.

I was ready.

I found my lighter and held the flame to what remained of my sage bundle. I blew on the bundle to extinguish the fire, encouraging the embers into swirls of smoke. After smudging from my head to my toes, I held the bowl before my heart, between my thumbs, to allow my palms to join in prayer.

I stepped from the east into the medicine circle, faced the same direction, and thanked the shield for the lessons of the spirit. I turned to the south and thanked the winds for the lessons of adolescence. "I thank Mouse for her survival skills and Coyote for his joyful yipping and zest for the hunt."

I turned west, blew on the sage bundle to encourage the smoke, and spoke to the winds. The sun was below the mountains; only its residual glow remained. "I ask the west to help me find purpose," I stated to the universe. "I ask Mountain Lion for her cunning and to share her hunting skills." I also asked Wolf to share her abilities to orchestrate the pack to take down prey much larger than their more diminutive canine stature.

Then I turned to the north and thanked the salmon and bison for their sacrifice and for feeding the village. "Winds, help me find worthy people who appreciate and deserve my talents."

Finally, I turned to the east and said aloud, "I open this circle; may it protect all those inside it, and may Spirit share with me only what I am ready to receive." With that, I sat down in my stone circle.

As with all ceremonies, the experience was subtle. No flashing visuals or LSD hallucinations appear on a mystic blackboard to provide lessons to the seeker. The night wind whistled, reminding me it would keep me company, and I wrapped my wool blanket around me.

I wished that Bandit, my personal spirit guide, would keep me company one last night. I pictured her ears perking up, eager to collect the sounds and waves of interest and guiding her agile spring toward her next destination. I told her I loved her, offered thanks for her vigilance, and looked back at the mountains. Their silhouette was barely visible; the only defining theme was the absence of stars below a jagged line along the horizon. Below was darkness; above was a sapphire tapestry filled with stars.

Time passed and passed, and the cosmic wheel turned across my celestial ceiling. I sat upright, tightened my wool cap, and blew on my hands. I was cold even through layers of thermal underwear, outerwear, and gloves. My blanket offered a placebo of warmth.

I looked east again, and Orion was there, high enough to guide me to Sirius, below and to the right, following the line formed by the three stars of the constellation's belt. The sun was coming. The night would soon retreat before our solar father crested the mountains to the east.

I thanked Orion and remembered a project in my first year at university. I chose the constellation as my topic and spent a night in a farmer's field, slowly photographing the cluster of stars. The slow exposure revealed each star's unique color. Some were blue, some were orange. On top of the photograph, I placed an acetate sheet that overlaid the names of the stars and drew lines to connect the dots that formed the constellation.

It seemed to me now that Orion encompassed the color palette of the desert. I thought about those lines and how an arrangement of finite dots could be connected by a few lines to form a hieroglyph durable enough to survive millennia. Its design lent meaning to numerous cultures, some now lost to time.

I thought about the connections. And it clicked: I was a connector. I could see distinct images in a field of random dots. I could tune out the noise and enhance the signal to provide meaning to those who could not see it themselves. That was my purpose. I was a *connector.*

I could arrange concepts to create a bigger-picture view. My meager upbringing ensured that I was always conscious of practicality. I could break down complex ideas into simple components, such as milestones, without losing sight of the bigger picture. I could help people navigate by reading my stars. It was a gift. It was my medicine.

Throughout my career, I have taken technically complex ideas and boiled them down for laypeople to understand. Once these ideas were stripped of jargon to reveal their meaning, people understood. I could use those milestones to create a framework or a path to a larger objective. How many times had I created a simplified matrix, helping executives understand the risks their businesses faced, and built a bridge between the technical experts who understood what needed to be done and the business leaders who had the authority to make it happen? I was able to bring them together.

I had often mused in talks that we needed a Rosetta stone to translate the ones and zeros of technology to the dollars and cents of business. I was that Rosetta stone. I could speak multiple languages to translate more effectively. I could bridge the language barrier, but I could also weave new ways of looking at challenges.

I was a connector. Like the Rosetta stone, I was lying in the desert, awaiting discovery.

I had found my purpose. I shuffled around to face the west again and thanked the unseen guides who had revealed my vocational constellation of understanding. My final ceremony was complete. When I returned to the world, I would need to find a worthy community that valued my ability to connect ideas to reveal hidden truths. I would later discover that not everyone can handle the truth.

CHAPTER NINE

From Solitude to Community

Death Valley, California, Day 9

The sun's arrival heralded the close of my solo time. I performed my morning ritual once more, meditating on my visions, but my thoughts were rushed. I was impatient to pack up and head back to our base camp.

After packing, I had one more task to perform before leaving my solitude. I needed to incorporate what I had learned and experienced. It was an after-action analysis of the visions I had received. In reality, incorporation is not a simple prayer or observance. It is a long process of processing, evaluation, and eventual integration.

At its essence, incorporation is the yang to the yin of severance. I discarded that which I wished to leave behind. Now, I needed to consider what I wished to carry forward. Pulling out my notebook, I unfolded my weathered letter of intent.

"In this second half of my life, I wish to incorporate my spirituality," I read aloud. "To do so, I must integrate humility and an openness to learn." After all, I was a novice at this, as Darkness had made clear. I was at the beginning of what could be a lifetime of learning.

"I will follow my heart, and do what is right, and trust those who truly love me, regardless of how my life's circumstances change." I thought of my daughter and the hard choices we would face soon, which would either bring us together or tear us apart.

I untucked my medicine bag from underneath my sweater. I bent down and picked up a small piece of rose quartz. I polished it between my thumb and index finger. It was cool and tingling. Then, I placed the small stone into my medicine bag. In return, I laid the remainder of my sage bundle in the sand from which I had taken the stone.

I took a deep breath and cleared the tears from my eyes. Today was the day I returned from my wilderness quest. More importantly, I was taking the first steps of a much longer journey.

Before stepping into my medicine circle for the last time, I smudged. When I was done, I put the abalone shell and feather on my altar. I faced the east. "Great spirits of the east, I thank you for creation. I thank Eagle for her vision, and I thank you for hearing my words and helping me leave this place closer to light and love."

I turned to the south and said aloud, "I thank you for passion. I thank you for helping me face the shadows of my childhood, which I carried through my adolescence. And I thank Coyote, who, like my brother, reminds me to laugh, even in hard times."

I turned to the west and continued. "I thank you for the

lesson of purpose and for finding my place in the flow of life. I thank you for helping me see my medicine.

"And to the north, I give thanks for my village," I said as I turned northward. "Thank you for helping me understand what it means to belong and to contribute to the community."

Returning to face the east, I looked up. "Thank you, Grandmother Moon, for looking over me, and Grandfather Sky, for shining your stars to keep me company." I looked down. "Thank you, Mother Earth, for providing and sharing your riches during my vision quest."

"With gratitude, I close this ceremony." I stood with my eyes closed, feeling the breeze on my skin, the heat of the sun, and a sense of resolve. Something had shifted in me, and I felt healed.

I opened my eyes and began the breakdown of my temporary home. I gathered the stones that had formed the perimeter of my camp and medicine wheel and tossed them around randomly. I picked up the smashed watch pieces and threw them over the east cliff. It was an offense to the "take nothing, leave everything as you found it" edict, but this one transgression felt right. I could have buried the watch or scattered its remains across the butte's side, but it was as lost as if it were six inches under the topsoil.

I was giddy with excitement. I had survived my solo time in the wilderness. Today, I would walk back out of the desert toward food and loved ones. I looked around one last time and started walking off the mount, leisurely knocking over the cairns I had placed to mark my route. As I descended, I tossed the quartz crystals from my camp back into the sand.

I returned to the flat and headed north toward the base camp, where I would find those who would accept my medicine. I had trekked for about half an hour when I crossed the familiar dried-out riverbed. I stood, debating whether to hike up to our stone pile to dismantle it. I tried to rationalize leaving it. I was tired, after all. A small stone pile lost in a desolate place that disliked human intrusion was barely recognizable as a human artifact in this land. I grumbled to myself and turned to head up the riverbed.

I came to the rockfall and found what remained of the stone pile. My partner had knocked it over as he passed through. I shook my head and turned back north to rejoin my fellow travelers.

As I hiked across the barren flats, scrambling through washout after washout, I spotted another person hiking ahead. I could make him out only as an iota in the daylight. *That must be Sam,* I thought. I hurried my pace to catch up. Days of surrendering left my ego antsy and ready to resume control. I increased my pace again, determined to beat my competitor back to the rendezvous point.

A few minutes into my sprint, I tripped into a washout and fell face first in the sand. I spat dirt and tiny twigs from my mouth and rubbed my lips to wipe the spit from my chin. I climbed to the rim of the washout and sat down. I was winded. If I continued at this increased pace, I would run out of fuel before I made it back to the group. My partner could take the victory. I did not have the strength for another challenge.

After a short rest, I struggled to my feet and continued walking north. Another forty-five minutes of unending, ever-stretching sand flats later, I stepped out of the desert on the first leg toward integration. I was on the road back.

Sparrow Hart welcomed my return with a hug. I fell into his embrace and let him take my weight. After a moment, I stepped back and uttered a raspy, "Thank you."

The travelers who had arrived before me lined up to offer welcoming hugs and congratulations. Once my reception was over, I dropped my pack beside my rental car and opened the doors to let the heat that had built up inside escape. A burning wave of trapped air exhaled from the vehicle like a dragon's breath. I sat on the tailgate for a minute, feeling free of the weight I had carried into the desert.

When I rejoined the group, Sparrow Hart had prepared a bowl of Muslix and fruit as my reintroduction to food. It was fresh and delicious. It was more than delicious—it was almost electric, like the touch of hypersensitivity on newly freed skin. I sipped deliciously cool water and waited to greet the remaining travelers as they returned.

Nearby, other travelers were swapping stories. We looked like prisoners of war on liberation day. Our jubilation was buried under a layer of dirt, our own bodies' filth, and the effort of days of fasting. To the ordinary person, our stories would have sounded like tourists competing to determine who had seen the most attractions. To us, it was a means of preserving our memories and testing their authenticity. It was real. We had gone into the desert and returned.

"I set up a mesa in the east, and found the entrance to a mine," Nancy, the elder woman in our group, announced. She looked proud, like a treasure hunter who returned with a bounty.

"Did you go in?" I asked.

"Not a chance!" she jabbed back. "It was a square opening in the top of the mesa, with a rickety old ladder that descended into the darkness." I shivered. The darkness was not to be trifled with. I had learned that firsthand.

"And you did not want to climb down," my fellow Canadian, Kevin, jested.

"The ladder was ancient," she explained. "Maybe it was from the 1800s. If I fell in, or the ladder broke, you guys would never have found me."

"You would have become another relic down there," I joked.

"Hey, kid—watch it!" she retorted and punched my chest. She took my comment as a swipe at her age. I swayed with the mock blow. It would not have taken much force to knock me back in my weakened state.

"What about you?" Kevin asked Sam, the retired financier.

"I had to move camp after the first night. I was up in the western mountains. The storms were washing me out. So I moved down into the valley south of that black butte," he said, pointing south to my temporary home.

"I was camped on top of that butte," I said.

"Really?" he responded. "Well, I found a circular group of big boulders. And there were broken pottery, and hieroglyphs." Sparrow Hart had mentioned that a shaman once graced the area. I had been so close to finding it, I thought. I guess I wasn't ready.

"Yeah, well, I had coyotes circling me one night," Ophelia, the young woman in her thirties, announced.

"Shit," I said in shock. "I saw paw prints around me but never *actually* saw anything. I did see a rattlesnake," I added to the amazement of the crowd. "I almost stepped on the damn thing."

Sparrow Hart stood nearby, listening but far enough away to avoid intrusion. This was part of our reintegration process, and he served as a guide, not a participant.

Once everyone had returned and eaten their fast-breaking meal, we returned to our cars to drive our caravan north out of Death Valley to our campground at Baker Creek. I was antsy, wanting to speed up to get home sooner. One bar of signal on my phone would occasionally appear to tease the chance of speaking to loved ones. I decided to wait until we got back to Big Pine.

When we returned, we looked like survivors of the apocalypse, filthy, worn, and ragged. Sparrow Hart gave us the rest of the day off.

"I am going into town. Does anybody want anything?" I asked the group. Some of the others were also going into town.

"I would love a boiled egg," Ophelia said.

Sparrow Hart strongly warned us against eating solid food too soon after fasting. "Your digestive system cannot handle it. You might get cramps, or worse," he warned. "Stick to soft foods like yogurt and fruit." Sparrow Hart was right, of course. Later that day, Kevin drove into town and gorged himself on McDonald's. For two days, he paid the price for his hasty gluttony.

But a cooked egg seemed harmless enough. "Okay. I will see what I can find," I replied to Ophelia. "See you in an hour." I headed to my car.

I drove to a gas station in Big Pine. It was a dilapidated building with metal shelves that seemed exhausted from holding their wares and buzzing fluorescent lights that looked to be one flicker away from their last. The place was crowded with junk food, fishing gear, hunting supplies, and automotive essentials.

First up, I called home and told my family I was safe.

"Did you see any scorpions or mountain lions?" Rebecca asked.

"No, but I stepped on a rattlesnake!" I shouted back, in a tone that made the gravity of the situation more cartoonish.

"That's crazy, Daddy. Did it bite you?" Rebecca asked.

"No, it was a nice snake, and it left me alone," I revealed. She seemed relieved and said, "That's good, Daddy. They are poisonous, you know. I saw it on *Wild Kratts*." She was referring to a children's television show about outdoor adventurers.

It was good to hear her voice, like a beacon back to the real world. She was light, and my reason for returning. More importantly, she was still there in my life. Darkness had not taken her from me.

"I love you, DD."

"I love you too," she responded.

"Okay, give the phone to Mommy."

After some banter back and forth with her mother, it was obvious to both of us that we were finished. There was no animosity, simply an unemotional recognition of the obvious.

I also called Michelle. When she answered, I said, "I'm back," in a matter-of-fact tone. I was hiding my exhilaration. I was alive, and in addition to my daughter, Michelle was the person I wanted to tell.

"Is it you?" she asked. The trepidation in her voice was apparent.

"Yes, I survived," I responded. At once, we felt reconnected, like lost friends and strangers meeting for the first time. Had she changed, or had I? Perhaps I was not the only traveler on this journey. Perhaps the observer was also altered by the experience, akin to a quantum mechanical transformation.

She asked about the trip, and I glossed over the details. I told her about seeing my dog, the darkness, and how cold it was at night, along with a few other details.

"I'm coming back," I announced. "See you soon."

After ending the call, I paid for shower tokens, retrieved my toiletries and towel from the car, and headed into the showers. They were what you would expect: a cinderblock structure of dividers, mildew, and dirt. Still, it was cleaner than I was. Cleaner than anything I had experienced in days. I washed my face with steaming-hot water and shaved before I stripped and slipped under the spray.

The water was medicine. With my first token, I removed the layers of dirt and sweat, like rings of a tree, falling away to reveal the age of my solo journey. I had been dirty for too long; my layers of filth proved it. The second token was decadent. I stood in the hot shower, shaking and crying. I luxuriated in the warmth of the falling water.

I was stripping away more than dirt. I was being reborn, baptized in this truck-stop river. I did not know who I was, and there was no Eddie Vedder soundtrack, just the sound of domesticated falling water. But in that moment, I was shedding the skin of the old to reveal the new.

I savored every drop until the timer systematically shut off the shower. I let the water run off me until I was nearly dry, then dressed in a fresh set of hiking clothes and returned to the gas station to purchase two hard-boiled eggs for my companion before setting off for Baker Creek and my fellow travelers.

Big Cedar, California, Day 10

In the morning, I climbed from my tent and made coffee and a package of instant oatmeal using my Jetboil stove. I struggled to swallow while eating. My glands had swelled and blocked my throat. I could not swallow the solid food. Luckily, one of my fellow travelers was a nurse. Nancy examined me, pushing on my glands and neck. "I think your saliva glands are blocked," she said. "It's common when people stop eating."

She explained the swelling was due to a crystalline blockage because the glands were not producing and excreting saliva as they usually would when I ate regularly. She felt around my neck again. "The blockage will slowly dissipate," she said. She smiled and slapped her hands against her legs. Her brown hair was speckled with dirt, which matched the brown of her freckles.

"In the meantime, don't eat solid food to avoid choking. Food might get lodged in your esophagus." I thought of my father and his esophageal cancer.

It seemed my fast had not finished with me, and I ate Lipton soup and yogurt for the next two days.

The next order of business was reconvening our wilderness group to facilitate reintegration. We passed the smudge bowl around and sat, cleansed by the sage smoke and shaded by the sequoias and bristlecone pines along Baker Creek. We shared our discoveries and solo-time stories, as if testing the waters and dipping our toes in before submerging ourselves fully. Over time, we each revealed something more profound.

I don't wish to share too much about what the others discovered. Their stories and quests are theirs, not mine. Like mine, their experiences were raw. What brought them to the desert, what they found there, and what they chose to carry forward with them was personal. I can offer only a myopic interpretation that cannot do their stories justice.

But here is one peripheral story. A middle-aged gentleman, Glen, had retired early after decades of serving a well-known technology firm based in the heartland of tech: San Jose, south of San Francisco. Now in his late fifties, he was a songwriter and guitarist of enough caliber to perform live in bands playing bar circuits. He was frustrated by an audience ambivalent to his offering. His band would play popular cover songs to tourists and students at the local colleges.

He expressed his frustration with an audience that seemed more interested in drinking, chatting, and hooking up than in music. He said in a bar of two hundred people, maybe ten or fifteen would crowd around the tables in front of the stage, singing along to his performance. They would call out, imploring the band to play their favorites so they could dance to the hits.

"Why should I bother when only a handful give a shit?" he lamented.

I do not know whether it was exhaustion or whether my emotional skin was rubbed raw. Either way, I'd had enough of this guy's self-pity, and I let him have it.

"You are so full of shit!" I unloaded. "Fuck you." I finished my one-two verbal punch. He was staring at me. Everyone was. No one moved as they waited for what came next. "I dream of performing onstage; I've spent years practicing guitar and singing." I delivered my next barrage. "I would kill to be in your place. You've retired early with enough money to live comfortably, and all you have to whine about is that some college kids are more interested in getting laid than listening to you cover Lynyrd Skynyrd and Pearl Jam?"

I shook my head and broke eye contact for a moment. Still, no one moved. Sparrow Hart was alert and watching. I could feel his eyes transfixed on me.

"Fuck you," I repeated, buying myself time to plan my next move. "No, fuck them!" My second wind filled my sails, and I was preparing to broadside this prick. "Fuck the ungrateful trust-fund kids, and play for your audience. Play for the people who came to see you. They came to see *you*, man! They made the *effort* for *you*."

I took another pause to gauge his reaction. Out of the corner of my eye, I could see as much as sense Sparrow Hart's gaze. Glen was listening.

"Play for the people who care, and fuck those who don't," I declared. "Play for your people. They are your *people*." I repeated, "They are your *people*. You found them!" I petered out: "You found them."

I slung my head and stood up, walking away from our circle. "I'm sorry," I muttered as tears filled my eyes. I was not sure why I was so upset, but I had struck my own chord. I stood facing the stream and the hill I climbed every morning.

I heard someone coming up behind me, and I turned to find the guitarist standing there. I was not sure what he would do.

"I'm sorry, Glen. I don't know why I reacted that way." I apologized, but my thought went unfinished. Years later, I would know.

"It's okay," he responded. "Thank you." I tried to ignore my tears as I met his gaze. "No one has ever said anything like that to me before. Not even my wife. Not my family or friends. No one."

I started to apologize again before he interrupted: "Do not

apologize. That was exactly what I needed," Glen said. "You made me see what was right in front of my face. Right in front of me." His people had been there the whole time, receiving his medicine, and his shadow of loss closed his eyes to the fact that I had punched him.

We stood for a beat and walked back to our place in the circle. When we returned, I apologized to the group. Nancy put her hand on my outstretched leg. Then another said, "Wow, man, you have a way with words."

I chuckled. "Yeah."

Sam spoke up. "I just hope you don't punch me like that when I tell my story." We all broke into laughter, which cleared the clouds of uneasiness and returned us to the safe space in which we could share our stories.

Why had I reacted so violently to Glen? Was I envious of his musical talent? No. Was I jealous of his financial freedom? Not enough to react that way.

And then it hit me. I was angry that he had found his people, a group that embraced his talent. That was it. In my career, I had always delivered but somehow felt undervalued. I always said the companies I worked for never understood what they had until I left; it was only then that they recognized what they'd lost. How could I get them to see what they had, before I was gone?

In an instant, it came to me. That was not my job. My job was to deliver the medicine, and theirs was to receive it. I needed to find my own community, like the guitarist, that appreciated my offering. I had won the lesson of the west, but I still had work to do in the north.

We continued around the circle, telling our stories and listening to reciprocal interpretations and advice. It was empowering to listen to people who were like me and were willing to share their secrets in a group of trust. When it was my turn, I focused on my experience with the darkness. I described how nothing came until the following day and how I lay paralyzed as my parade of Dickensian ghosts came one at a time to show me what I feared to see.

I recounted the feeling of helplessness as my spirits stripped me bare. I knew what mattered, who I could not lose, and what I had to do. I had found my purpose, my medicine, and now I had to find the community to receive me and my gifts. It was clear the corporate world I was in was happy to take my gifts as long as I was willing to give. But they were not willing to reciprocate.

I had a friend who used to say that your life balances on three legs: your career, your family, and your health. You can handle one being out of whack, but two will topple you. I knew that my marriage was dissolving, and my career was about to change course—two legs wobbling. Maybe it was time to get up and kick over the chair before it fell and hurt me. It was time to make a new life. This one was dying. It needed to be severed before I could find a new path.

Let the bridges I burn light my way, I thought. I was glowing in the light of the newly anointed. Rather than a peaceful warrior, I sounded like a fundamentalist or a radical. I was wobbly as I tried to stand in the energy of an emerging life.

After our circle had dispersed, Nancy called me from her encampment by the creek. I hopped over the burbling water and sat in a camp chair that she pointed out. She was a kindly lady in her seventies, divorced, and a longtime empty nester. She had spent her time traveling, most of it alone. She had some wisdom to offer me, tempering my radical intentions and giving me another perspective.

"There are no winners in divorce, kid. Only survivors," she said. She fished a cigarette from its package, turned away from me, and lit it with a well-used Zippo lighter.

When her gaze returned, she let out a puff that foreshadowed her next words. "Before you mess with other people's lives, figure out your own shit first."

Nancy was as much begging me as warning me. In that moment, I knew she had been on the receiving end of something similar. Alternatively, she had made a rash decision without understanding the consequences.

"Get yourself straight," she continued. "Then deal with the people around you."

Listening to her, I thought about the Breitling watch I had smashed to sever an unhealthy bond. I had considered the consequences. I had weighed the costs and the gains. I was definitive in my actions. Severing a marriage was not as simple as smashing a material object. Unlike my watch, people had feelings, and experiences shaped their perceptions. A single moment could ripple through the rest of their lives.

"Thanks," I said. She sat in her chair, more interested in the remains of her cigarette than our conversation. She'd said her piece, though both of us knew I had already made up my mind.

"I am going to go back to the group." My words lilted as I spoke.

"Yep," she replied. She had dismissed me, just as she likely thought I had dismissed her advice. As I walked away, I looked back. She had her legs up on a nearby tree and was staring across the creek.

"Thanks," I muttered again. I know she did not hear me. But I had heard her.

I knew divorce was the right decision. But now, I would tread with compassion. A righteous path will always be there, no matter how long it takes to walk. After all, you often find your fate on the path to avoid it. If divorce was right, it would happen. And in its proper time.

The next morning was the group's final day together, and we prepared for reintegration into society. Sitting in his old shirt and cargo pants, just like he had before our solo time, Sparrow Hart was again our guide. "You are not who you were," he explained. "And people are often afraid of who comes back."

He cautioned that many would not recognize us or would fear the change. Our shift in vibration would affect theirs. They would have to face their truths as a consequence, or they would build a cactus-like defense to avoid hearing our message.

"You will find you are frustrated by everyday life. People at the airport will be extra annoying," he said. "Or standing in line at your grocery store will seem pointless." We did not understand how valid his words would be.

Even the tempo of everyday life would seem offbeat. We had discovered something more that rendered consumerism and corporate life a pointless exercise and a waste of time. Once you taste Source, you will never be satisfied with a plastic-water-bottle version of life.

We each packed our equipment into our cars and, one by one, said our goodbyes, making promises to remain in touch. We would break those promises. Our time together was complete. We had served our communal purpose.

I climbed my hill one last time, to visit the cairn I'd built to Eagle all those days before. In a windstorm, the head and wing stones had toppled away. I pushed the remaining rocks off the top of the hill, said my thanks, and walked back down to leave.

Las Vegas, Nevada, Day 11

I retraced my route through the mountains into Nevada and back to Las Vegas, which stood as the gates to the real world. I arrived on the Strip in late afternoon and had time to kill before my red-eye flight home. I decided to eat dinner at an upscale Italian restaurant I had previously frequented during conferences in Vegas.

Though I had cleaned up the best I could in the Big Pine

coin shower, the look of the maître d' told me I belonged in a zombie movie as an extra or perhaps an escaped prisoner in some war movie. I was clean but looked too wild to inhabit a fine-dining establishment. But this was Las Vegas, after all. Money was money, whether it was the loose change of a wealthy diner or the rent payment of a poorer one. He seated me at the end of the bar, beside the kitchen entrance, probably to limit any potential contamination.

The bartenders eyed me with skepticism and whispered to one another. Was I a vagabond who would hit on a slot machine or an eccentric millionaire who liked to dress like a survivor of the apocalypse? If the tip were sufficient, I could be whoever I wanted.

That was the result of a society that traded real for fake. Money mattered, no matter what the currency was backed by. The backstory was worthless in a world that valued the ends and excused its means. The other diners made sure to avoid eye contact with me. They wore expensive cotton suits and shiny dresses that dangled off their tanned shoulders and breasts. Their jewelry flashed their arrival. They were made people, living it up in this adult playground of excess. I was a ragged blemish to be ignored. I finished my linguine del mar, licked the last drop of Barolo from my wineglass, and paid—I could sense the waitstaff's relief. I slipped out quietly and headed to the airport.

Right before boarding, the gate attendant spoke into the PA system. "Attention, passengers on Air Canada Rouge flight 1704 to Toronto, we regrettably announce that the flight is canceled."

As the attendant continued with instructions and promises of compensation, the crowd complained and broke into a cacophony of one person speaking over the next.

The plane's cockpit windscreen had cracked on landing. The western winds had fought hard and come out the better. I had faced numerous delayed flights in my travels, but this felt different. It was as if the world was rejecting my return. I was a foreign body to be expelled.

I thought about driving back to Big Pine and never going home, but I could not abandon my daughter. She was precious. She deserved better. I was her rock, and she was mine. I would not abandon my people the way my father had.

After hours of frustration and running between airline counters, I hopped on a flight to San Francisco. From there, I had a direct flight home to Toronto. When I arrived in San Francisco, I checked in at the counter and was told I was too late. I would spend the day in SFO, waiting for another red-eye home that evening. I was done with this world that rejected my every attempt to return home. I took my new boarding passes and shuffled toward the delay with disappointment.

I sat at a group of tables in the middle of the international terminal and cried. I was spent. I could not survive another day in the wilderness. I placed my head down on the table. Other passengers must have thought I was just a weary traveler who had suffered a temporary breakdown brought on by the unreliability of modern air travel. Most likely, they thought I was drunk. After all, airports existed free from the constraints of time. Seven o'clock in the morning was as good a time as any to drink.

I felt a nudge and the weight of something resting against my leg. I opened my eyes and saw my dog, Bandit, sitting beside me. "Hello, old friend," I murmured as she laid her head in my lap. I rubbed her side, the silky warmth of her fur soothing me. We sat together like that for a long time. I knew I would be all right. I knew I would find my way back out of the wilderness.

CHAPTER TEN

The Inner Ember Rekindled

Kitchener-Waterloo, Ontario, 2025

I emerged from the desert and divorced Rebecca's mother. Not right away. But eventually. Like all divorces, it ripped apart the community we'd formed. I lost friends, neighbors, and even family members who could not understand why I had taken that stupid trip, as if it were to blame for my resulting divorce.

Through it all, I feared losing my daughter, but she is still with me. She escaped that childhood room, crying herself to sleep, listening to her parents arguing downstairs. I did not lose her or live a fake life for her. She did not change her name to erase her ancestry or cut me from her life. We remain close.

I fondly remember Nancy, the nurse, and sometimes think of her smoking that cigarette while staring into the wilderness.

The eddies of smoke were a reminder that she was right. Divorce is a hard road, and it should be a last resort, not the first exit when things get tough. Luckily, in our case, all parties did more than survive, even if they were a little scarred and worn by the experience.

Years later, I married a woman I came to love deeply. Before my wilderness quest, Michelle gave me a medicine bag as a symbol of faith and a means to carry what was important to me. In 2019, she gave me her hand in marriage. We bought a house together, merged our families, and planted a large maple in the east corner of our yard.

"This is our family tree," Michelle explained. "It will grow with our family if we nurture it." At last, I had found my people. They loved me, and I them.

The tree stands vigil, a reminder that seasons come and go. Storms might rage and rain will fall, but a tree with strong-enough roots will endure. As the tree in winter trusts in the coming of spring, I am learning to trust. Each day, I root deeper with my loved ones. The moments of beauty, which I call "glimmers," build my trust in others. As I drop my defenses, I am rewarded with love.

I changed jobs a few years after I returned from the desert to focus on writing, research, and speaking. I specialized in connecting disparate groups, people, and concepts. It culminated with the job that ended just before I began writing this. Like the seasons, not everything lasts.

The tree does not change into something different between winter and summer. Instead, it alters its form and focuses its energy on what matters to survive. When things are lean, it sheds its leaves and hibernates, waiting for spring. The tree is the embodiment of the medicine wheel, containing all four shields, none of which is more important than the other. No one season is more important or better than another. It's just different.

As I write this, I am experiencing a professional winter, but I still have my voice, and I can still read the constellations. My job is gone, but not my medicine. Nothing can take that from me if I do not surrender it. As I had with Darkness, I must honor its force and negotiate a way of living with the shadow times in my life.

Even without my old professional community, I am still the connector I was. It's time to find a new community—that's all. I am no less an expert or talented orator than I was when on conference stages. Like Glen, I am financially stable enough to semiretire and work contract roles until I find my next opportunity. Like Glen, I need to find the few who are there to listen. It is time for me to find my new audience.

It is time to find a new stage.

—

Reflection on my time in Death Valley reminds me to follow my path. I recently found the medicine bag Michelle had given me, buried at the back of a bedside drawer. It still contained the stone I'd taken with me from the desert. It was a small heart that beats even now, sitting on a west-facing windowsill of my home office.

I think back to feeling the warmth of the rising sun after a cold night. Nothing compares to the feeling of connection to something greater than yourself. Connection at its simplest implies the existence of more than one thing, be it a person, an inanimate object, or a tree. It suggests that belonging in a community is a higher state of being than solitude. The problem is that the modern, technology-driven collective has robbed us of authenticity. We relish the glow of a tablet screen instead of the warmth of the sun.

Beyond a prescribed path through life, modern society draws us away from Source. I was terrified before I set foot in the desert. Now, I see the desert (and any wilderness, for that matter) as a refuge from the real danger. Unlike society, the desert does not camouflage its antagonism. The cactus is a sharp, harsh survivor. You do not have to touch its prickly branches to know it is something to avoid. Animals and insects dressed in bright colors announce their hazards. It is an aposematic wonderland of danger. So how do thousands of animals, insects, and plants flourish? Because they do not disguise their perils. Natural guardrails give a warning to help keep inhabitants safe. Our civilization puts up guardrails to restrict our direction of travel.

We have traded the dangers of brightly colored insects and snakes for the perceived safety of our neon-lit prison. Our world is designed to lure its prey, one small purchase at a time. It is a world of "keep off the grass" landmines, when what we should be doing is taking off our shoes and grounding our feet in Mother Earth.

I often wonder how the human mind keeps up with technological progress. Our parents didn't have computers. There was a small base of knowledge to attain in school. When I was a teenager, I had to call my girlfriend on a corded phone and survive the inevitable interrogation of her parents to connect with her.

Now, people meet online. They establish rapport without ever meeting in person. They use proxy questions designed to cull the herd and identify potential mates. My older daughter told me that she asks "Pancakes or waffles?" to test suitors. One guy replied, "Pussy." Is this our culture now?

We live in a house of mirrors, bombarded by cognitive distortions served up in bite-size social-media posts. Truth is gone. Fact is fiction. We value celebrities and athletes over doctors and teachers. We trade proxy for intrinsic value. The band Radiohead certainly had it right with their song "Fake Plastic Trees." The lyrical protagonist cries for escape from the ubiquitous fakery of his life. We prefer artificial nature to walking among the genuine article.

Did Ian Fleming have it right in his James Bond novels? Are the billionaires the true villains, determined to stop at nothing to amass everything? Is excessive wealth parity to ethical bankruptcy? If so, is poverty pious, then? How do we ascertain truth, build values, and find our path in a world that pulls us further away from what truly matters? The fact that we cannot answer these questions should tell us what we need to know.

How do you fan your inner ember when the nine-to-five life tries to extinguish it? The inner ember is a compass, a guide toward Source and the things that matter.

When I told Michelle I was writing this book, she asked me, "You learned so many things about yourself in the desert, but where does it appear in your life now?" She was not accusing me of ignoring those dusty lessons. She was trying to draw out examples of Source and make me think about how it can enrich our lives.

I will never forget a flight home from Orlando in the summer of 2024. On that occasion, I arrived at the airport gate early. I was lined up in the first boarding zone, a privilege I'd earned, with nearly a million loyalty air miles in my account.

A woman lined up behind me with her child seated in an airport wheelchair. He was no more than ten. Disney pins, Mickey Mouse, superheroes, and pastel princesses adorned his bag. He wore a special Disney lanyard and Mickey Mouse ears. I smiled at his mother. The boy's father approached and spoke quietly to his wife. I looked at the boy and then back up at his mother.

"Excuse me," I interrupted. "You know, you can preboard. You don't need to line up with the rest of us." His mother thanked me as his father rifled through his carry-on bag. He seemed distracted by something he had misplaced.

"You can go in front of me," I offered. The boy's father

stopped looking through his bag and pushed his son forward as I stepped out of the way. His mother conveyed her appreciation again. His father nodded his gratitude. The silence was awkward. Nature abhors a vacuum, and I rushed into the space, attempting to dispel the uneasy moment, unaware of what would come.

"How was Disney? Did your son enjoy his time?" I asked.

"Oh, he loved it," his mother responded as tears welled in her eyes. I was confused and embarrassed that I had made her uncomfortable with what seemed a benign attempt at small talk. "He's on a Make-A-Wish trip." She barely made it through the words.

I felt horrible. What started as small talk had exposed the most significant loss of their life. The boy's father turned away to hide his tears. The mother told me they were returning to the hospital when they landed. She said it in a way that made me understand this was a one-way trip for the lad in the wheelchair.

I was instantly a little boy again, listening to my father and a doctor tell me that my newborn brother would not survive. The loss was crushing. I had no words, only remorse for making this moment more painful. As I stood speechless, a flight attendant ushered the family up the jet bridge. It was a small mercy.

I stood there, swimming in their pain. It had been Orlando from which I'd returned when I'd kept my brother company while he died in the hospital. I understood, in my way, the path they were about to walk. It was a slow and agonizing journey that did not guarantee recovery. I said a small prayer and fumbled with my passport when the gate attendant called zone one to board. I was holding up a line of impatient travelers.

As I sat in business class, I thought of the little boy on his way to the great beyond and his parents, who would be left behind, unable to fill the space of their son.

I thought of my aunt and the children with incurable diseases she treated. She was either their savior or their executioner. She saved those she could and eased the passing of those she could not. She was a surgeon triaging the wounded on the battlefield, surrounded by blood, pain, and loss, knowing that not everyone would make it. Nevertheless, she persevered into her late seventies before retiring.

My aunt reminded me that even in darkness, there is light. She showed me how to see the light, no matter how dark our lives become. Perhaps you cannot fix a person's failing health or take away their worries. However, you can choose not to add to them. Hold a door for someone who needs help. Look up from your smartphone, and look at the world around you. Take up a hobby you enjoy. Add to the light in the world instead of making it darker.

My darkness showed me light. My father ran from his fears and cowered in a bottle instead of doing better than his forebears. I do my best to face my challenges. My brother gave me the gift of compassion. Furthermore, my mother taught me that you cannot make someone choose you. That is their decision to make. Yours is to grow your gifts. Purpose and gratitude are the only way to complete the sacred hoop. It is the path back to Source.

Finding Source is the human urge to find existential purpose and return to the divine. If we discover our bodily purpose in the west and live it to fruition in the north, then we return to the east, our souls closer to Spirit.

Society's purpose is so close, but we have lost the essence of Spirit. We attend college to discover our role and secure a job that allows us to share our gifts with an adopted village. On the surface, both paths seem to track back to Source. Yet our modern highway has lost the soul of the dusty trail our ancestors walked. Societal values are on the right track, but they often condone antithetical means to justify their end. The purpose is so often insincere, and the village is there for its own gain, at the cost of its villagers.

In pursuing life, we can find meaning, take forward the good, and leave behind the bad. Every year, this exercise seems more challenging as we become increasingly confused and distracted by life. Extremists compete to outshout one another. The immediate gain of cruelty has replaced the reward of doing what is right, even if it is harder or takes longer. Society separates instead of uniting us. Society distracts us with sports, polarizing news stories, and the next phone or car purchase. It's just noise. We mistake it for the signal when it is more akin to the static on a detuned television.

The best way to tune in is by listening to your inner ember. It is a purity that cannot be bought or placated with a new car or bigger house. It glows when you do what is right, and it aches when you move away from Source. That is why people ignore their inner embers. Its pang is a cry to do better. Yet "better" is often more arduous. Not everyone is ready to commit. Immediate gratification is a powerful analgesic.

Over the last decade, I stopped listening to my ember. Through the unexpected loss of my job and writing this book, I found the quiet to hear its voice again. I found something divine in the desert. I found the solitude to listen to myself. I delineated between what I needed and what I thought I wanted. It has taken years to return to that place.

Now, I am grateful for what I have instead of lamenting what I lack. Gratitude feeds your ember. A colleague once asked me, "What do you do when you reach the top of the mountain?" At the time, I responded, "I look for the next mountain to climb." Now, I enjoy the view from where I happen to be.

I have slowed down enough to disconnect from the world. I got off the highway to take the scenic route. It might be slower, but the view is worth the delay. I no longer take little things for granted. I find light in the small moments, like floating in the pool on a sunny day, watching football on a Sunday with the family, or sitting by the fire on a quiet evening.

We wake on warm summer mornings and sip coffee while reading by the poolside. I watch Henry, our small white dog, float in the pool. He sprawls on a cobalt-blue floatie meant for an adult. The water cools his belly on hot days, and we place a sun hat over his head to protect his eyes from the blinding rays. He sleeps as the floatie drifts around, pushed by a gentle breeze. Henry is an old dog who spends most of his time sleeping. Be like Henry. He floats with the current.

On still summer evenings, I walk over to a clutch of cedars where I buried my border collie, Maggie, who passed several winters ago. I still miss that girl and cherish our time together. I stand in the cedars and speak to her. I was not always as patient as I should have been. Dogs ask very little in exchange for so much. They need a little patience, and in return, they give unconditional love. I relish the time with our new puppy, a gorgeous black Lab named Nessie, after the Scottish cryptid. Nessie is pure joy. She loves everyone and everything. She is a direct connection to Source, undistracted by life. I remember Maggie's lesson about finding the patience to let an unbridled puppy run free.

The fire crackles, and I recline in an Adirondack chair, watching the flames dance in our firepit. Wisps of smoke and embers ascend to blend with the night sky. I follow their trail to gaze at the stars and watch the planets traverse the sky. I bask in the warmth I have found.

I remember my desert poem:

> *The two forks of this river come together when*
> *they are meant to and never before.*
> *They must each carve out their path to form a*
> *deep Sapphire Lake where they eternally*
> *unite.*

Our family had carved out their own identities and become one. In reverence to our journey, I adorned the front of our house with a brass sign that reads Sapphire Lake House.

I still struggle to listen to my inner ember sometimes—it is an ongoing journey. The cacophony of our lives drowns out the whisper of what matters, and we have to work to hold on to that.

My wife holds us true with a bedtime ritual. Every night, lying in bed with the lights turned off, we hold hands and share our gratitude.

"What are you grateful for today?" she asks.

I respond with little glimmers of light, like moments with our new puppy or something nice that happened that day.

She tells me what she is grateful for. We hold hands and fall asleep like otters floating in a river.

Acknowledgments

I thank Sparrow Hart for sharing his medicine with our group as we sought healing from our wounds, and for Spirit, who gave Sparrow Hart the message atop the holy Black Hills of South Dakota.

I thank my wife, Michelle, who bravely waited for a man she cared deeply for until he was capable of accepting true love. I thank her for her fearlessness in reading my manuscripts (which could not have been easy) and keeping me fed and watered as I experienced what I can only call a download from Source. For weeks, I searched for words in a desert of my office. She kept me tethered to this world and our home.

I thank my daughters, Rebecca and Lauren, for their love. I thank my extended sons, Liam and Carter, for their support. I am grateful to my living and dead animal companions for their unconditional love.

I also thank Death Valley's animals, rocks, stones, sky, and sand. This place taught me to live with the land rather than on it. Last, I thank my inner ember, the light that always keeps me on my path.

Selected Works

I am in no way an expert in North American Indigenous cultures. This list of curated readings contains the books I studied before departing for Death Valley. These books offer details about Indigenous cultures, including their beliefs, rituals, and ceremonies. This list also includes books and movies that I drew inspiration from. It's by no means a comprehensive list. But like my spiritual journey, they were totems from which I found comfort. I hope they give you what you seek, be it knowledge, motivation, or a spark for your ember.

Andrews, Ted. *Animal-Speak: The Spiritual & Magical Powers of Creatures Great & Small*. Llewellyn Publications, 2002.

Benton-Banai, Edward. *The Mishomis Book: The Voice of the Ojibway*. University of Minnesota Press, 2010.

Black Elk, John G. Neihardt, Vine Deloria, and Phillip J. Deloria Jr. *Black Elk Speaks: The Complete Edition*. University of Nebraska Press, 2017.

Eanes, Russ. *The Walk of a Lifetime: 500 miles on the Camino de Santiago*. The Walker Press, 2019.

Estevez, Emilio, dir. *The Way*. Icon Entertainment, 2010.

Gilbert, Elizabeth. *Eat, Pray, Love: One Woman's Search for Everything Across Italy, India and Indonesia*. Riverhead Books, 2007.

Hart, Sparrow. *Letters to the River: A Guide to a Dream Worth Living*. CreateSpace Independent Publishing Platform, 2013.

Hart, Sparrow. *The Vision Quest: A Guide's Training Manual.* Published by the author, 2019.

Ing, Dean. *Pulling Through.* Ace, 1983.

Krakauer, Jon. *Into the Wild.* Anchor Books, 1997.

Lane Jr., Phil, Judie Bopp, Michael Bopp, and Lee Brown. *The Sacred Tree: Reflections on Native American Spirituality.* Lotus Press, 1992.

Levy, Paul. *Dispelling Wetiko: Breaking the Curse of Evil.* North Atlantic Books, 2013.

Nabigon, Herb. *The Hollow Tree: Fighting Addiction with Traditional Native Healing.* McGill-Queen's University Press, 2006.

Plotkin, Bill. *Soulcraft: Crossing into the Mysteries of Nature and Psyche.* New World Library, 2003.

Rusho, W. L. *Everett Ruess: A Vagabond for Beauty.* Gibbs Smith, 1973.

Strayed, Cheryl. *Wild: From Lost to Found on the Pacific Crest Trail.* Thorndike Press, 2013.

About the Author

MARK SANGSTER is the author of *Cyber-Conscious Leadership: A Practical Guide to Protecting Your Organization Against Cybercrime* and *No Safe Harbor: The Inside Truth About Cybercrime—and How to Protect Your Business*. He is an award-winning speaker and has presented at international conferences and prestigious stages, including Harvard Law School. Mark has appeared on *CNN News Hour* to provide expert opinions on international cybercrime issues and is a go-to subject-matter expert for leading publications, including *The Wall Street Journal* and *Forbes*.

www.ingramcontent.com/pod-product-compliance
Lightning Source LLC
Chambersburg PA
CBHW030921060726
47591CB00005B/1621